THE MAKERS.

THE MAKERS.

Inside the homes and studios of inspiring creatives.

Hardie Grant
BOOKS

By Bed Threads.

RENOVATIONS & BUILDS 172

FAMILY HOMES 228

COUNTRY ESCAPES 262

LETTER FROM THE EDITOR

Genevieve Rosen-Biller
Co-Founder, Bed Threads

You never forget your first home. Let me tell you about mine. It was tiny. *Tiny*. A one-and-a-half-bedroom apartment that was so small the bathroom was split into separate parts: toilet in one little cubicle, and shower in another. The hot water only ran for seven minutes. The living room, dining room, kitchen, workplace and laundry – it was all one room.

Still, it didn't matter to me because it was mine. I loved how it had high ceilings with an ornate, antique pattern that circled the lights. It was north facing with beautiful natural sunlight that made everything seem so bright. My mum is an artist and she painted some pieces that made the space feel like a home. My biggest decorating splurge was going to the market every weekend to buy a fresh bunch of flowers. I loved coming home in the evenings and I woke up feeling so happy every day that I lived there.

Let me tell you something else about this apartment. This was the space where, in 2017, my husband Alan and I came up with the idea for Bed Threads. When we were trying to decorate this space, we realised very quickly that we were priced out of having beautiful, quality products for our home.

When I looked around for inspiration, I didn't see the kind of space I was living in – and really loving living in! – reflected at all. I didn't see any celebration of setting up your first apartment and decorating it in a way that reflected your personal style. I didn't see

any tips or advice on how to craft interiors within your means. I didn't feel like there was anywhere I could shop for quality pieces that reflected my aesthetic and environmental standpoint, and that were also accessible to me.

If you're reading this book, I imagine you already know what came next. Alan and I started Bed Threads out of our spare room, where we were trying to create something for all the people like us searching for ways to make their spaces *theirs*.

Fairly soon after we started Bed Threads, we began publishing a series on Sunday nights called *The Makers* to our Journal. In it, a creative person opened their home to us and let us into their space, sharing tips on how to decorate, design and hone your personal style, while sharing their interior and career journeys with us.

This series has become a flagship of our brand, which is why we decided to put *The Makers* into print. This book contains more than 50 of our most beloved home tours, near and far, Australian and global, from podcaster and writer Pandora Sykes to artist Lauren Freestone and content creator Courtney Adamo, whose gorgeous 120-year-old Northern Rivers family home is one of our most popular to date. In this book, there are chic city rentals and rambling country escapes, and, of course, a whole section dedicated to people in their very first home, creating their dream space – however that might look for them.

INTRODUCTION

Whenever we think about the concept of home, there is one overwhelming emotion that we feel: peace. For us here at Bed Threads, home should be a place where you truly can be yourself, whether you're entertaining, sleeping in, or relaxing on the couch after a long day. Home is about feeling calm, at ease and relaxed. It's about knowing that whenever you step through your front door, you can exhale – because you're home.

It's why we feel so privileged to make products that become a part of your everyday routines and rituals. The linen sheets on your bed, the towels in your bathroom, the tablecloth and napkins in your dining room, the throws on your sofa, the art on your walls. Here at Bed Threads, we know that creating a home that gives you that sense of peace (and, hopefully, joy!) is important. And it's a journey we love being part of with you.

Long-term followers of Bed Threads will know that *The Makers* is our name for the home and studio tours we have shared with our community on our Journal for many, many years. It almost dates back to the inception of Bed Threads. *The Makers* was created to celebrate the home in all of its various forms, sizes, locations and life stages. It's a way of showing that your home is yours, a personal space for you to curate exactly as you want to.

One thing we have learned over the years of producing *The Makers* – and being invited into the private homes of creative people all around Australia and the world – is that there is a strong link between creativity and your personal space. It's not possible to be creative and to think clearly without a sense of peace within yourself. And one of the truest ways to achieve this is a space in which you can be (and express) yourself. Somewhere you can retreat to and relax in, away from the outside world, without judgment or scrutiny. Your home.

Encouraging that sense of peace and, in turn, that creative force, is one of the reasons we first started producing *The Makers* all those years ago. Now, following on from the success of our first self-published book *Put On A Spread*, we are so proud to bring you *The Makers* in print, a selection of more than 50 of our most inspiring home tours from over the years. Whether it's the colourful first Sydney rental apartment of content creator Rowi Singh – remember the lilac shag rug? – or Pandora Sykes' quirky and playful Victorian terrace in London, *The Makers* is about celebrating individuality in design and the ways we choose to make our houses into homes.

Every one of our home tours is unique, because they are a reflection of the unique personality of the creative who has welcomed us into their space. Each of these stories serves as a reminder that there really is no such thing as the perfect home. There is only the perfect home for you. When you start to design your own home, the most important thing you should be striving for is comfort. Fill your space with the things you love, the art you admire, the furniture you covet and the design accents you obsess over. Your home should feel special to *you*. And the only person whose opinion matters is yours.

We hope this book serves as a reminder to listen to your taste, follow your instincts and, most of all, to have fun when decorating. No matter where you are in your life – you might be in your first apartment, your forever family home, your city pad or your country escape – your dream home is possible. As long as it's uniquely yours.

RENTALS

Rather than being stifled by the limitations that come with a lease, these resourceful creatives have made their rental homes truly theirs. From Loui Burke's linen-clad city pad to Rowi Singh's dreamy technicolour digs, these thoughtfully curated spaces show that your dream home can truly be wherever you are now.

ROWI SINGH

*A striking space filled with colour
and eclectic finds makes the perfect first home
for this talented content creator.*

At the beginning of 2020, Rowi Singh and her then-boyfriend, now-husband Rahul Sharma made the leap: they got a place of their own. The apartment, in the inner Sydney suburb of Redfern, is "pretty humble and not flashy at all", Rowi says. But the content creator – you'll find her making colourful beauty looks at @RowiSingh and celebrating BIPOC creatives at @TheArtives – loved the fact that the flat was minutes away from her best friends and in the heart of such a vibrant neighbourhood.

 This apartment is Rowi's first home of her own – previously, she lived with her parents – so she approached decorating it with care. "Don't rush to fill your place for the sake of it," she advises. "Collect pieces you love by curating a moodboard, doing lots of research and hunting down secondhand pieces where you can." Rowi knows that it is decoration that helps a rental become a home, especially when you can't make any major changes or renovations to the space itself. As she says, "[Our apartment is] very unsuspecting from the outside. But we've elevated it and made it our own with colourful finds, both new and old."

 One such colourful find is the squishy green velvet sofa which sits pride of place in the living room – Rowi's favourite room in the flat. It's where her unique and eclectic taste is on full display. There are artworks by Nick Thomm on the walls alongside specially commissioned skateboards from Rholtsu, a cult favourite twisty neon candle from Jolie Laide on a gold and glass side table and a thick shaggy rug covering the floor. Over in the bedroom, Rowi has her accessories – resin sunglasses, chunky gold earrings – stored in perspex containers, and colourful turmeric and lavender linen on her bed.

Content
creator

•

Redfern,
Sydney, NSW

13

You can see Rowi's taste everywhere. The space is cool, striking and full of life, just like the incredible makeup looks she creates online. "I love turning my ideas into a visual showcase of who I am as a person. My content is unapologetically bold, colourful, culturally infused, edgy and abstract. It's freeing to break from typical standards of beauty and style to bring something completely refreshing to the table.

"My home is very reflective of myself, my partner and my art," she says. "It's super fun and colourful. Like I did with my makeup, we threw the home-decor rulebook out the window and just went for what makes us feel happy and motivated." Mission definitely accomplished.

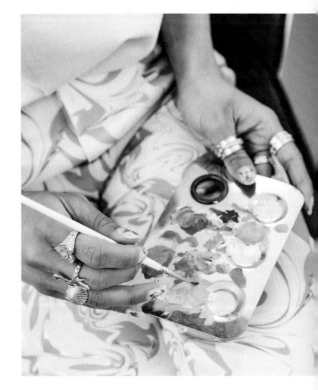

"It's super fun and colourful. Like I did
with my makeup, we threw the home-
decor rulebook out the window."

17

FLEX MAMI

*This technicolour dream home
in Sydney's inner west is
bursting with style and personality.*

Ghanaian-Australian Lillian Ahenkan (aka Flex Mami) is so much more than one of Australia's favourite influencers. Sure, she's got tens of thousands of devoted fans on Instagram, but Flex is also a business woman, bestselling author, DJ, podcaster and furniture designer. Now, though, she's focused on being more "behind the scenes", she says.

She admits that having an online presence can be difficult. "[It] requires solid mental health, resilience and understanding of trends, and a commitment to sharing every single part of yourself."

They are skills that have no doubt served Flex when building Flex Factory, the online store where she sells her popular 'ReFlex' conversation card games and a collection of homewares including prints, cushions, scarves, coasters and plates.

"I'm really interested in using the skills I have to continue to build product-based businesses, as opposed to selling myself," she explains. "I still want to be online, I still want to be building a relationship with my audience, but as it stands I think I'm far more driven to build something more tangible that exists outside of me."

Flex says the best thing about running her own online store is being able to conceptualise exciting, unique and creative ideas and see them through to fruition. "All of my bizarre iPhone note brainstorms are becoming a reality and I am honestly so stoked," she says.

In 2021, as well as publishing her first book *The Success Experiment* – revealing her 'formula for knowing what you really want and how to get it' – Flex also moved into her new rental in Sydney's Dulwich Hill, a technicolour dream home that's bursting with style, colour and creativity.

"[When styling the interior] I definitely chose to go the clean maximalism route," she says. "I've already lived in a smaller space that had knick knacks on every possible surface, but in this new space I wanted it to feel far more serene and relaxed and not as busy. So I've purposely tried to fill the space with pieces that pack a punch."

Podcaster
+
Author
+
Entrepreneur

•

Dulwich Hill,
Sydney, NSW

19

"I definitely chose to go the clean maximalism route – I've purposely tried to fill the space with pieces that pack a punch."

When she first moved in, Flex loved that it was a blank canvas that she could fill with her favourite pieces, including a bright yellow banana rocking chair and a side table that's a circular pane of glass sat atop a white tiger head.

Flex is a big fan of DIY – "Honestly, I just make what I can't buy, because it doesn't exist or it's too expensive," – but says some styling must-haves include beautiful bedding that sparks joy, bright and coloured LED lighting, a few key pieces of artwork, and rugs!

YVONNE STARR

*An earthy palette combines with vintage pieces
to bring life and personality to this special home.*

When it comes to sourcing secondhand homewares, Yvonne Starr has an exceptional eye for detail. After running out of space in her own home, Yvonne launched her thoughtfully curated vintage furniture business, Ukitu, as a means to share her pre-loved passion with other interior enthusiasts.

Meaning 'touched' in Basque, Ukitu sells everything from fossil stone consoles to antique ceramic urns via limited drops on Instagram. Her loyal community excitedly awaits each specially curated drop, which almost always sells out within seconds of going live.

Still, if you thought her feed was envy-inducing, wait until you see her home. Set to an earthy palette of beige, tan, terracotta and natural wood, there's a beautiful consistency and flow throughout the space. A lover of texture, Yvonne weaves spectacular secondhand cane and rattan pieces together with contemporary artwork and unique sculptural vases to create a modern-Mediterranean-meets-vintage aesthetic.

"I source, restore and breathe new life into pre-loved furniture and wares," explains the mother of three, whose hobby developed into a career. "I was uninspired by the conventional homewares and furniture on the market, so I started sourcing secondhand pieces for our own home and found that they were much more special and unique. I continued to source and swap things around my home and then began to run out of space, hence Ukitu being born!"

Yvonne's home is light, welcoming and full of personality and design. "Being an apartment, you have to work with the space you're given and you don't have a lot of creative freedom when it comes to the structure. So, we worked with what we had – light walls and floors – and dressed them up with quality and pre-loved wares and furniture. I think it's important to spend money on some pieces you love, but not everything needed to be designer, so we filled in the gaps with handmade or vintage," she says.

And her favourite room in the house? "The living space oozes with my favourite neutral and warm tones, a lot of texture, sculptural pieces and raw material, and is the best place to sit back and enjoy a cuppa! I feel inspired and relaxed at the same time."

Vintage
enthusiast
+
Founder of Ukitu

•

Sutherland,
Sydney, NSW

"The living space oozes with my favourite neutral and warm tones, a lot of texture, sculptural pieces and raw material, and is the best place to sit back and enjoy a cuppa! I feel inspired and relaxed at the same time."

JOSH AND MATT

*Experience the magic of colour inside
creative duo Josh and Matt's playful
inner-city apartment.*

You know that saying: "This is where the magic happens"? Well, it's certainly true for this apartment in the middle of Melbourne's CBD, the home of Josh & Matt Design, an art and homewares partnership run by this super creative couple.

The pair moved to Melbourne in February 2021 and fell in love with their inner city flat because of its space to create, soaring windows and second-to-none views over the city. "When we saw the curved windows in the living area capturing the views of Melbourne, we were completely sold," the pair explains.

The social media-famous duo spent their time at home during the lockdowns of 2021 creating all the pieces you've seen on their Instagram and TikTok – candles, artwork, homewares, wall hangings – all rental-friendly, colourful and full of fun.

Now, Josh and Matt share that they have never felt more at home. The couple have filled the space with a cacophony of colour, art and design: pink clay and turmeric sheets from Bed Threads, twin squidgy red Togo armchairs, a 1993 Vilbert chair, a Memphis Milano squash tray and a custom desk from Curated Spaces. There's also countless objects and pieces sourced from Instagram, vintage stores, Facebook Marketplace and fellow designers.

"Making to us has always been about reflecting who we are," they say. "We really enjoy experimenting with materiality and colour, which has allowed us to create quite a diverse range of home decor. We both have quite playful personalities, which is reflected in the designs we create.

"We don't worry too much about making sure everything fits a specific style, it really is just a blend of a lot of different eras and styles meshed together with our own flair."

That being said, no matter which room you're designing, Josh and Matt advise making a moodboard for your home broken down into the following categories: colour, materiality and form. "This will help you find unexpected decor and furniture pieces that tie into the style you're aiming for," they say.

Their top tip? Always look up. "Your ceiling is often forgotten but it can really help balance out your room. Creating a focal point draws the eye up, making your room feel taller and larger than it is!"

Designers

•

Melbourne CBD,
Victoria

29

"We both have quite playful personalities,
 which is reflected in the designs we create."

They also advise being open to change and improvements to your original ideas: "Don't get too attached to your original designs. The design process is often a windy road and isn't always straightforward, so the sooner you allow yourself to be open to change, the quicker you'll create your best version."

31

MADELINE JOVICIC

This creative's playful apartment
feels like a sunny European holiday.

Step inside Madeline Jovicic's Sydney apartment and the sounds
and sensations of a European summer holiday instantly come alive.

The Australian artist's playful and whimsical painting style –
with references to street food, sardines and gelato stands – directly
translates into her home's interiors. Just take her living room as an
example. If you picture yourself sitting on her fresh white bouclé
armchair with her sand-coloured rug, a gallery wall of her own pastel
paintings and natural sunlight beaming in through the open glass
doors, you could almost be relaxing beachside, indulging in scoops
of gelato and sipping on limoncello.

But it's not just Madeline's living room that awakens
a sense of yesteryear's holiday. The travel nostalgia overflows into
her bedroom, fitted with sweet peach and golden turmeric linen
sheets, an Ionic column-shaped bedside table and her own gelato-
inspired painting.

Madeline spends her mornings in her art studio – the apartment's
second bedroom – sketching and painting ideas that come to mind, while
afternoons are spent out in the courtyard – one of her favourite places
in the apartment – soaking up the sun, sometimes with an aperitif in hand.

She shares the challenges and joys of turning her creative passion
into a business: "I often find myself way out of my comfort zone, which
is scary but important for growth. Every time someone buys something
that I've created it's still so surreal to me. The best part is being able
to wake up and do something I love every day," she says.

Madeline has come a long way in turning her plain white-walled
apartment into a holiday fantasy brimming with personality.

"This apartment is quite generic and modern, which isn't my style
at all," she says. "So my goal has been to fill it with items that bring
in some much-needed warmth and character to the space. It's definitely
still a work in progress, but I like to take my time with adding pieces
as I find things I love."

Nonetheless, this creative's humble flat is proof that even the
smallest of spaces can be transformed into vibrant living, working and
entertaining spaces that feel just like a holiday.

Madeline shares her tips for a well-styled home: "For me,
it's all about surrounding yourself with objects that make you happy,
comfortable and inspired. I love the act of collecting and curating pieces,
from op-shops to boutiques, and even overseas travels."

Artist

•

Rosebery,
Sydney, NSW

"Every time someone buys something
that I've created it's still so surreal to me.
The best part is being able to wake up and
do something I love every day."

35

ALLIRA POTTER

This relaxed sun-soaked home, filled with light, plants and colour, doubles as a haven for yoga, meditation and spiritual practice.

Teacher, guide, coach, activist. Meet Allira Potter, a Yorta Yorta woman living in Geelong who incorporates First Nations practices and knowledge into her work as an energy healer, meditation teacher and psychic. Host of Mamamia's wellbeing podcast Fill My Cup and author of *Wild and Witchy*, Potter is bringing mindfulness, wellbeing and spirituality to a new generation of Australian women.

Though Allira has always been deeply spiritual, her career as a practising healer began a few years ago after completing her reiki training. Having previously worked as a model, photographer and creative content producer, taking her work into this realm has been more about recognising – and then finding her way back to – her true calling. Now, Allira shares her guiding gifts with thousands daily.

"I make people happy!" she says, "But no, seriously, I am a multi-faceted human. I am an energy healer, meditation teacher, sassy psychic, Aboriginal activist, and life coach in the making.

"I am a spiritual human and, being Aboriginal, it's in my blood to be connected to my mind, body and spirit as much as possible. I think my personality is pretty loud yet grounded, and I'm not afraid to stand up for what I believe in. I think the act of making relates to my personality because I love giving back as much as possible and I love being able to help people where needed."

Throughout her sun-soaked space, sage and incense burns on loop, while crystals, tinctures and magical remedies line surfaces and shelves. In her bedroom – her self-described 'haven' – a floor-to-ceiling window floods the room with natural light, while luscious potted plants bask in its glory.

Healer

•

Geelong, Victoria

Throughout Allira's airy abode, original artworks by First Nations artists take pride of place (and wall space!), which add depth and colour to her impeccably styled home. Here, among subtle hues of apricot, terracotta and pine, Allira has created a relaxed and tranquil space that feels both cosmically calming and aptly awakening at once.

"My style is pretty eclectic. I love bright things but love my furnishings to be either grey or timber so that I can decorate with all the colour," Allira says. "My favourite room is my yoga, meditation and healing space. The images speak for themselves – it's the space where I not only host my business but also rest and relax."

"I am a spiritual human, and
being Aboriginal it's in my blood
to be connected to my mind, body
and spirit as much as possible."

LOUI BURKE

The talented stylist has made over his inner-city rental
with neutral tones and natural textures aplenty.

Content creator and creative director Loui Burke says it's his star sign that defined his creative journey. "I'm a Virgo sun, Taurus moon and Capricorn rising," he says. "So essentially, I love to organise everything, be extremely comfortable, very proactive and practical. Which I feel like best explains me and why content creation and design is where I ended up."

While the zodiac might be the driving force, it was also the years Loui spent working in his family's hospitality business, studying creative direction and design, and eventually becoming a stylist and creative director for a childrenswear and bedding brand that gave him the expertise he has today. "I learnt all about the layers that go into making up a beautiful space," Loui says of his various jobs. "All the small details that feel inviting and special."

An urban-loft-style apartment was something Loui had always dreamed of living in, so as soon as he found this space in Melbourne's Docklands, he knew it was for him. The zen home presents a successful homage to wabi-sabi, the Japanese philosophy of finding beauty in the imperfect. The building's industrial warehouse design is warmed up by neutral tones and a materials palette of timber, jute, linen and hammered brass.

"What it lacks in colour, I like to think I make up for in texture," he says. "I love how calm the space feels. The amount of room I have is amazing and the high ceilings are awesome. The industrial old-world shell with all the rough edges and large beams just brings so much interest and added texture that complements my style."

Despite the home centring around a pared-back sense of design, there are unique details scattered throughout that make it feel special. These include a painter's ladder bought from a warehouse in Richmond, bowls from local brand Made in Japan, and crystal-glass candleholders from India. "I'm always on the lookout on Facebook Marketplace for secondhand treasures," he shares.

And what about his advice for a beautiful bedroom? "Layers!" Loui exclaims. "And lots of them. Always start with a good foundation of rugs, curtains and bedding. Then, your furniture pieces. They don't have to be super expensive, because once you layer in bed linen, blankets and books you've got one beautiful set up. Also, go into designing your space knowing it's going to take some time. Enjoy the process!"

Creative
director

•

Docklands,
Melbourne, Victoria

41

"I just love the contrast of that clean urban cityscape with a more rustic, honest look and feel."

CAROLINE WALLS

*The artist's calming Victorian terrace
is not only a home but a space that allows
her the freedom to create.*

Renowned for her minimalistic renderings of the female form, Caroline Walls has made a name for herself as one of Australia's most prominent and revered contemporary artists. Her recognition represents the movement towards a more gender-inclusive art world.

After completing an Honours degree in Visual Communication, Caroline worked for a number of years in fashion art direction and design at lifestyle brand agencies in New York and London. She later returned to Australia where she completed postgraduate studies in Visual Arts before continuing her practice from her studio in Melbourne. She has presented nine solo exhibitions, over a dozen group exhibitions, and her art adorns an array of stylish homes, cafes and retail stores.

Caroline's portrayals of the feminine form are intimate and carefully observed. "I tend to explore ideas, experiences and feelings that have touched me personally as a woman, such as fertility, motherhood, sexuality, intimacy, desire and the need for emotional connection," she says.

In the same vein as her artworks, Caroline's affinity for muted, earthy tones permeates the interior of her home in Melbourne, which she shares with wife Emma Hill and their two daughters. The calming residence is restrained in its palette and styling choices, functioning as a warm sanctuary for the young family and a place for Caroline to create.

"I've looked to find a balance so that I can still enjoy a space that highlights my love of art and neutral tones," she says.

Texture, shapes and a layered palette play a key role in the success of this home's aesthetic which would otherwise be lacklustre with such little variance in colour. The incorporation of a sisal rug, rattan chairs, and ceramics in the open-plan living/dining room inject the space with warmth and visual interest, while handsome charcoal linen in the bedroom ties in elegantly with the bold, dark accents seen throughout the home's decor and Caroline's charcoal drawings.

Artist

•

Northcote,
Melbourne, Victoria

45

Caroline's love for art is showcased throughout the abode with a carefully curated selection of works in the form of sculptures, paintings and turned-timber pieces.

"These pieces are placed throughout our home in various places, above fireplaces, layered on shelves and so on. I continue to grow my collection which includes objects made by local makers and serendipitous charity-shop finds," she says.

The overall look is inviting and tasteful with a calming ambience that's ideal for an artist to work in.

"It's hard to say which is my favourite room as they all bring me a lot of happiness for different reasons, but I really do love my new studio which has views across the inner north of Melbourne through to the city skyline which has this expansive and open feel to it. This really inspires me so much when I am creating, and the ever-changing view throughout the day is so beautiful. I love to watch the last of the day's sunshine when the sky is warm and glowing and the city lights start to twinkle."

"I've looked to find a balance so that I can still enjoy a space that highlights my love of art and neutral tones."

SACHA STREBE

*The chic apartment of this Australian
editorial director and creative consultant
melds international style with a nomad vibe.*

There's a little bit of everything in Sacha Strebe's Los Angeles home.
The apartment, in the trendy neighbourhood of Silverlake in the city's
east, is a glorious mix of all of Sacha's and her husband's individual
tastes. There's a little California cool (mid-century modern chairs,
crystals galore), a little of the relaxed, beachy Australian vibe (pale wood,
lots of greenery), and there's even a touch of Europe – courtesy
of an antique painting in a stunning gilt frame, Diptyque candles
and one big, show-stopping timber column in the bedroom.

"We are travellers at heart," says Sacha, a seasoned editorial
director and creative consultant who has been at the helm of respected
titles such as *EyeSwoon*, *MyDomaine*, and *Create & Cultivate*. Sacha
met her husband while backpacking in Nice almost 20 years ago,
and together they've brought that love of adventure all the way from
Melbourne, where they were previously based, to their current home
in Los Angeles. "I really wanted to bring that European sentiment
into the space, too," she says. "Who wouldn't want to feel like they're
in Italy while they're working from home in Los Angeles?"

Sacha moved into the apartment over six years ago. Securing the
apartment was a stroke of good fortune: the couple had spent a week
searching for places without much luck. This apartment popped up on
Craigslist and her husband went for a tour. "My husband is never early,
but he turned up at the open house way before the set time and was
the first person at the door," Sacha recalls. They fell in love with the
building and the neighbourhood, particularly the school across the
road that was perfect for their young son. Sacha, ever the storyteller
and editorial wizard, prepared a stellar renters' pitch – soon, the keys
were theirs.

Because they're renting, the couple haven't made any major
changes. "Although I'd love to gut the kitchen and bathrooms," Sacha
admits. Instead, they've focused on the decorative, collaborating and
working with local makers to create personal and unique touches
for their home. Sacha commissioned her friend Omar (he goes by
@nymphobrainiac on Instagram) to make a "beautiful birch timber"
bedroom suite, including a bed frame and bookshelf.

Editor

•

Silverlake,
Los Angeles,
United States

51

Then there's Sacha's self-confessed mild obsession with clay, pottery and terracotta vessels, which she searches for in antique stores.

She loves to spend time designing and redesigning her space, creating Pinterest moodboards and looking online for inspiration. Sacha's biggest tip for anyone trying to make their home feel as individual, specialised and unique as her apartment? "Make it personal," she says. "Really think about what you love and clearly define what you don't – that part is just as important!"

"Who wouldn't want to feel like they're in
Italy while they're working from home
in Los Angeles?"

JESSALYN BROOKS

*Treasures collected over the years, artworks
and items that spark joy have transformed
an empty studio space for this creative.*

Jessalyn Brooks has lived in this warehouse for years. Over ten "whopping" years in fact, in which she has transformed the sprawling space into a creative hub, both for her painting and other artworks, and for her life.

Over the past decade, the warehouse has undergone several major renovations, all courtesy of Jessalyn herself. "It was just raw studio space when I first moved in," she recalls. "[I] built all the walls, all that stuff. I used to work at an old architectural wrecking yard when I first moved in and the owner was kind enough to give me a bunch of junk to furnish my place with."

The fruits of Jessalyn's labours are easy to see in this warehouse, a combination of light-filled and paint-splattered empty space for Jessalyn to make her colourful artworks in, contrasted against the cosy and lived-in personal areas where she cooks, eats, relaxes and sleeps, all decorated with treasured items collected over the years. "Everything in this place has a little story and I love that," she enthuses. "Each piece of furniture – God, even my fridge has a funny story. Everything here had a life before it found me."

Jessalyn loves cooking: her electric Hotpoint stove from the '50s is her most cherished item in the whole apartment. It takes pride of place in her kitchen, underneath a big window and surrounded by tangled house plants and salvaged bits of antique furniture, forming part of the beautiful and unique tapestry of her personal space.

She's yet to add some curtains, though. "I've been meaning to get some really rad curtains in this place," she says. "I don't know why I haven't as it seems like such a simple task. Some beautiful linen curtains to filter the intense Los Angeles light would be so beautiful."

"Authentic connection with space, placement and objects is pretty important," Jessalyn explains. "My room is somewhat simple, but each piece brings me so much joy. Everything has intention and meaning."

For her bedroom, Jessalyn favours a neutral colour palette and sumptuous fabrics. "I love to be decadent and lush, so fabrics and textures are such a central part of my decorating. I like to imagine myself in a Lord Byron poem. I definitely prefer everything to be vintage – as they say, they just don't make 'em like they used to. It's pretty true. Except for Bed Threads, that is!"

Artist

•

Los Angeles,
United States

"Everything in this place has
 a little story and I love that."

JESSICA MARAK

Small DIY touches and a kaleidoscopic style make this playful apartment the ideal creative space.

Far from dreading being stuck in front of a computer all day, graphic designer, photographer and content creator Jessica Marak finds constant inspiration from her screen. "I wouldn't be the creative person I am today without the countless hours of sitting in front of a computer screen," she says.

"I always start on the computer, which is why I'm so grateful I chose the graphic design path. I can't create without it! When I'm buying furniture or picking out paint colors I'm in Photoshop. When I'm starting a branding project I'm in Illustrator. When I'm creating social content I'm in Premiere or Lightroom."

Jessica and her husband moved from New York to Los Angeles over a year ago, immediately falling in love with the arched doorways, casement windows and dark wood floors of their rented apartment.

In an effort to personalise the space, they swapped out all the light fixtures and gave a few rooms a new lick of paint.

"I created a moodboard, of course, based on a few themes including '60s modernism, Spanish warmth and playfulness. My husband Garrett and I love to have fun, so we wanted our home to be a reflection of that. We ended up with a lot of quirky shapes, rounded corners, and squiggles, but mixed in natural woods, marbles and sophisticated colours to balance out the playfulness."

Her collection of vintage coloured glasses takes pride of place within one of her favourite pieces: a post-modern stucco shelf in the dining room. "It was one of the first pieces we brought into the space and it fits perfectly. After living in such a small space in New York, it's such a luxury to have somewhere to display my collection." she says.

Most of her creative magic happens in the office/guest room. "I haven't had a designated creative space in so many years, so it feels so good to have a place where I can work on projects and make a mess and then close the door behind me."

And her secret to a well-styled home? "Fresh flowers. They add a pop of colour, but also give a whole new life and energy to the space. I love going to the flower market and buying really unique, out-there flowers. My favourites are push-pin proteas."

Graphic designer
+
Content creator

•

Los Angeles, United States

67

"I created a moodboard, of course, based on a few themes including '60s modernism, Spanish warmth and playfulness."

PUNO PUNO

*This light-filled loft transformed into
the perfect multi-functional home for
a passionate and busy creative.*

Puno Puno could be considered an internet jack-of-all-trades –
or a 'slashie', as she prefers to call it. In addition to designing websites,
Squarespace templates and nail wraps, the Los Angeles-based
entrepreneur produces videos, photoshoots and more on behalf of the
online resource-based community she created, ilovecreatives, as well
as clients such as Girlboss. "I love the process of creating," she says.
"Ideas are interesting, but actually seeing them take shape and form
is the most fun part for me."

When searching for a rental in Downtown Los Angeles with her
husband Daniel and their beloved cat Muad'Dib, they needed a space
that was versatile and suited to their work and lifestyle – part home,
part office, part studio, part co-working hub, part entertaining space,
and beyond. The two eventually landed on a 1,500 square-ft industrial-
style apartment with wall-to-wall windows, a cosy lofted bedroom,
and plenty of space to work remotely indefinitely.

They knew it was the place for them when they saw the windows.
"The windows! We get a ton of natural light. It was actually a friend's
place before we moved in – we kept asking when can we move in?"

Years later and the loft is basically a physical manifestation
of both ilovecreatives and Puno's brain. Filled with plants, pastels,
'70s-inspired furniture, and a few vintage Milo Baughman gems – a style
Puno refers to as 'Danish Tropical' – the space checks every box
on the couples' unique list of requirements. In addition to hosting
friends and coworkers, the space has served as HQ for ilovecreatives
for the better part of a decade.

Puno says her favourite pieces in the home are her pink
Daniel & Emma bar stools, with the Milo Baughman kitchen table
from Etsy running a close second. The bedroom is a warm oasis
of gorgeous peach and coral. "I painted the walls a coral colour
because I wanted it to 'glow', and that's what I love most about it.
With the peach and terracotta bedding, the room feels really warm."

Founder of
ilovecreatives

•

Los Angeles,
United States

"Ideas are interesting, but actually
seeing them take shape and form
is the most fun part for me."

NAM VO

*The beauty guru makes her home in
a chic loft apartment with a pared-back
colour scheme and comforting aesthetic.*

The need to create is in Nam Vo's DNA. The naturally gifted makeup artist and influencer has received widespread attention for her infectious personality and beautiful makeup looks, which she primarily creates in her minimal and ultra-chic New York City loft.

After dropping out of school to pursue a career in makeup, Nam went from working as a beauty artist at strip clubs to freelancing for magazines. "I always sucked at school but I was good at making friends and making girls feel pretty," she shares. Now, the much-loved beauty guru is renowned for creating her flawless and glowy 'dewy dumpling' makeup look on herself and her clients, which she masterfully shares on her Instagram account @NamVo.

This iconic dewy look, her natural ability to command an audience, and her love for sharing has garnered her thousands of followers. "Ever since I was a kid, if I ate pizza or a new candy I would tell everybody about it. And as an adult I'm doing the exact same thing, I just have a bigger audience," she says. Nam has also created her famous radiant skin look for the likes of model Rosie Huntington-Whiteley and established herself as a Global Artistry Ambassador for Marc Jacobs Beauty.

The pandemic was one of the driving forces behind Nam investing in a home that she loves and can comfortably work in. As a makeup artist, plenty of natural light was a must and the large arched window in the open-plan living/dining area keeps her New York City apartment looking fresh and inviting. The ultra-stylish living room is perhaps the star of the loft with its luxurious marble tables and curved bouclé sofas.

The home aptly utilises shades that mimic a dumpling. From the flooring to the walls, everything is swathed in warm neutral tones. The dialled-down palette, combined with curvaceous furniture and decor, creates a look that's utterly soothing and acts as a calming retreat and workspace. "My mind is very busy, and I'm a shopaholic so I wanted it to be clean," she says.

"It wasn't until this apartment that I truly loved every single thing in my home, every fork, plate, rug etc. I'm a very messy person, but I think when you work hard and you take pride in everything that you've bought, you actually want to take care of it," she says.

Makeup artist

•

Greenwich Village,
New York,
United States

77

The pared-back hues and comforting aesthetic continue in her loft-style bedroom which overlooks the dining space and can only be described as a 'glowy' sleep sanctuary. Here, white, oatmeal, beige and tan offer up a dreamy palette that is carefully curated to create the cosiest of spaces.

"My top tip is invest in the key pieces," Nam shares. "There are things you can go cheap on but the big statement pieces I would invest in. Keep it simple. There is so much good furniture around and you can get inspiration from Pinterest and Instagram, there's just so much. But I think you should just pick things that make you feel comfortable and relaxed."

"I'm a very messy person, but I think when you work hard and you take pride in everything that you've bought, you actually want to take care of it."

DECOR HACKS

Landlord-approved improvements you can DIY to make your rental your own.

While renting has plenty of benefits, one of its drawbacks is not being able to make substantial, lasting changes to a space in the way you'd like to. Often the biggest determining factors to how a place looks and feels – the colour of the walls, flooring, plus kitchen and bathroom fit-outs – are sadly the ones that are at the whim of your landlord. But that doesn't mean you're completely kept from making improvements.

Here are five clever ways to decorate your rental that even your landlord will love.

1.

INSTALL NEW BLINDS.

Changing the blinds or curtains is one of the simplest and most impactful ways to reinvigorate a space. If the place has existing fabric curtains that need a refresh, try swapping them for crisp white or sheer fabric drapes (just be sure to hold onto the old ones to re-hang before you go).

2.

SWAP OUT HANDLES.

If you have a screwdriver handy, you can easily switch out the handles on your kitchen or bathroom cabinets and drawers. Single-knob varieties are typically the easiest to update, while if your handles have two holes, unscrew them and remove the handle, then measure the distance between the middle of the two holes to find a fitting replacement.

3.

ADD AMBIENT LIGHTING.

In an ideal world, all lighting in your home would be adjustable by a mood-enhancing dimmer switch. But this is not an ideal world; it's a rental world, and more often than not you can be stuck with stark overhead lighting that does nothing for your home's ambience. Our advice? Replace any cool white bulbs for warm-toned ones, add a few free-standing lamps around the room (or update any pendant light fittings if they're not to your taste), and bask in the warm, inviting glow of your revamped rental.

4.

COVER UP WITH A RUG.

If the flooring 'situation' in your rental is unbearable, or you just want a refresh, a large rug is an easy fix and will likely remain useful well into the future. A neutral rug like a cream or tan jute is a good way to go, both because light colours will make the room seem more spacious, and because you can pick them up for a relatively reasonable price per square metre.

5.

DISPLAY SOME ART.

Hanging artwork is one of the surest ways to imbue a space with joy and personality, and one of the great things about building up an art collection is that it's forever yours no matter where you go. Use hanging strips to leave the walls unmarked, or if your artwork is on the heavier side, remember to patch and paint over any nail holes before handing back the keys.

CITY SPOTS

From Susan Alexandra's kaleidoscopic Lower East Side space to the ultra-zen Sydney spot where Zara Seidler gets out of bed to break the news, each of these urban oases reflects the style of the homeowner and the city they live in. Thoughtful touches and considered design choices help craft these small but perfectly formed spaces.

SUSAN ALEXANDRA

*Colour and creativity reign supreme
in this spirited apartment.*

Susan Alexandra has lived in seven apartments in New York City. "I have moved SO much in New York," the accessories designer jokes. Perhaps this one is lucky number seven. Susan received the keys to her current space on the Lower East Side in January 2021. "I just knew it this time," she enthuses. "I only saw this place and decided it was perfect."

She was won over by both the location - smack bang in the middle of one of the city's most vibrant neighbourhoods - and the bones of the space: cosy, good light and a blank canvas that the designer could add her own stamp to.

"I am renting, so all alterations to the space are superficial," she stresses, but that doesn't mean she has been unable to change things up in the apartment. Two of her major improvements were covering the kitchen cabinets in coloured contact paper "to make them more vibrant" and switching up some of the light fixtures. "This makes a world of difference," she says – and it's an easy and affordable quasi-renovation, too.

Susan's style is creative and full of life, as seen in both her apartment and her designs – such as her trademark beaded micro bags and eccentric charm necklaces. "I've always loved creating, since I was very little," she says. In the living space, an open shelf displays treasures and knick knacks, while a marigold yellow dining table from Wiggle Room and a collection of mismatched chairs stands in the centre of the room. It's her favourite room in the apartment: "I spend 98 per cent of my time here," she admits.

Accessories
designer

•

Lower East Side,
New York,
United States

There are a few more pieces Susan wants to add to her home. Some beaded lampshades, custom-made for the apartment by the designer, and a curved mirror. Collecting homewares is one of her passions, which is why she has launched her own range of interior decor pieces.

So, how would she advise you to approach styling your own space, to make it as exciting and full of life as her own? "My whole life revolves around making. I'm constantly seeking inspiration and ideas," she says. "I think lots of personal touches are what make any home stand out."

89

"I think lots of personal touches
are what make any home stand out."

VICTORIA JANE

*This whimsical home brings
a slice of cottagecore to the city.*

Victoria Jane's artistic talents are plentiful and she has embraced
a multitude of creative pursuits. The photographer, florist and set stylist
currently lives in New York City, creating still-life scenes for brands
such as Toby's Estate Coffee and Deux Cranes chocolates.

Victoria studied engineering at college before realising she wanted
to pursue a career that let her embrace her creativity. When working
as a part-time barista, she put her hand up to take photographs of the
cafe's food for their website.

"A true lesson I learnt is to always keep an open (and hopeful)
mind about where your next opportunity is going to come from!"
Victoria shares.

Her creative process is intuitive. "Some of my favourite work
stems from instantaneous, 'random' moments when I've spontaneously
decided to shoot," she says. "If I over-think, I tend to psych myself out -
so sometimes it's better to almost blindside myself."

Her rental home feels like a slice of cottagecore-meets-retro
heaven in Brooklyn and has been styled to feel as open and welcoming
as possible. A rotation of floral arrangements in an eclectic range of
vases can be found throughout the home, injecting each room with life
and colour. Botanical prints and vintage furniture also feature in each
room, playing into the homely aesthetic. "I want guests to come over
and to be able to enjoy the space to its fullest and relax!" she explains.

In the kitchen and dining area, barn-style hinges and timber
joinery with open shelving further play into the sweet, cottage-like
aesthetic of the home. Move to the primary bedroom and you are
greeted with lavender and lilac linen which adds a whimsical touch
to the space - a pretty, flower-inspired floor lamp and floral prints
complete the effect.

"I've become more thoughtful with what I bring and keep in my
home, which allows me to choose and style with pieces that feel truly
authentic to me," she says.

Photographer
+
Stylist

•

Brooklyn,
New York,
United States

95

Victoria is a walking example of following your gut when selecting the right space for you - particularly when it comes to aspects or pieces that you love and admire.

"It was all because of the yellow table in the kitchen. The apartment listing showed the space empty except for the kitchen, which had a bright-yellow dining table in it. I saw it and immediately asked the realtor, 'Does the space come with that table?' When she said yes, I knew this was the space for me."

"I've become more thoughtful
with what I bring and keep
in my home which allows me
to choose and style with pieces
that truly feel authentic to me."

CHRISTOPHER GRIFFIN

*Step inside this Instagram star's
leafy apartment and discover the
indoor jungle of your dreams.*

Botanical superstar and LGBTQIA+ activist Christopher Griffin, aka Plant Kween, lives in a plant-filled oasis in Brooklyn, New York, where they care for their "lil indoor jungle of over 200 green gurls". Back in 2016, they started their Instagram account, which now has hundreds of thousands of "equally plant-obsessed" followers, as a creative outlet to share the many lessons, lush adventures, and simple joys that come with being a plant parent. "My social media presence has been rooted in a journey of self-care, joy-sharing and community-building, all through the wonders of those green little creatures we call plants," they say.

Plant Kween also uses the botanical scene as a vehicle for larger conversations around identity: "I make digital content as a Black queer non-binary femme. I explore creative and accessible ways to use plants as a vehicle to incite further conversations centring Black joy and resilience, LGBTQIA+ advocacy and the need to increase the visibility, representation and empowerment of QTPOC (Queer and Trans People of Colour) in the lush world of horticulture."

When Christopher moved into their Brooklyn apartment, they were fastidious about preparing the home and positioning each plant to suit its individual needs. "I made note of all the various lighting situations, the walls that were drenched with that good ole ambient light, the corners that got a few hours of direct sun, those shady no-go areas," they explain. The apartment boasts five south-facing windows and is filled with more than 200 plants.

"It was a fun process that ultimately led to my green gurls continuing to serve lush lewks," they say.

Horticultural
expert

•

Brooklyn,
New York, United States

"My apartment is a love letter to my past,
present and future self and I'm taking my time,
writing it patiently, intentionally, and slowly...
enjoying all aspects of my process."

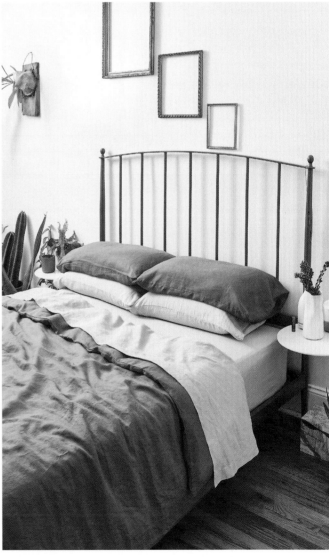

In the main bedroom, rust and sage linen sheets tie in perfectly with the indoor-jungle scheme. "I have to say it's been lovely waking up to a lil jungle of greenery every morning," they say of the 75 lush plants in this space alone. "My apartment is a love letter to my past, present and future self and I'm taking my time, writing it patiently, intentionally and slowly... enjoying all aspects of my process."

JESS TRAN

A light-filled warehouse is home to this
Australian creative and her collection of plants.

It was a frosty January day in New York City when Jess Tran first set eyes on her new home. The Australian creative had been living in America for about five years when she saw a listing for a split-level warehouse in Brooklyn with big windows, good light and lots of character.

"I remember walking in the door during magic hour, and instantly falling in love," she recalls. "The excessive amount of light, the ridiculous layout, the incredibly high ceilings... Even the fact that there was this decrepit vibe to it was attractive to me," she adds. "The whole place just looked like nothing else I had seen in my five years living in New York City."

Jess has filled the space with pots and pots of house plants, "a billion paintings", and reclaimed furniture. Given that she is renting, her one big renovation is purely aesthetic. "We did decide to install a fully functioning disco ball that lights up and spins when you say 'Hey Google, let's party'. I think that was a good decision."

Jess' interior style is colourful, eclectic, creative and cosy. She says she decorates by intuition. "I see what I need furniture-wise and then see what's available on Craigslist, vintage stores, Etsy, Facebook Marketplace, Chairish, TheRealReal and AptDeco," she says. "If the piece is a strong standout to me, and my partner signs off on it, the rest is built piece by piece as I find it. That's the magic of buying vintage and secondhand, you are a bit at the whim of the universe in terms of selection."

In the bedroom, contrasting shades of rust and sage Bed Threads linen sheets fit the warm and earthy colour palette that flows throughout the dreamy warehouse apartment. Some of her many plants are stored in planters picked up on overseas trips, such as the leopard planter that she found in Mexico City. "Pieces that come home with you from travel are always my favourite," she says.

"Plants warm up any space," she explains. "Elevated plants on different levels even more so." And now, after years of collecting, Jess is satisfied with the careful curation of design elements in her beautiful home, so much so that she has decided to halt new purchases for the moment. "It feels as complete as it needs to be for right now," she says.

Photographer

•

Brooklyn,
New York, United States

"Plants warm up any space. Elevated plants on different levels even more so."

TANTRI MUSTIKA

*A studio apartment reimagined
as an Art Deco paradise
in the hands of a talented ceramicist.*

When Tantri Mustika started viewing property "on a whim" in early 2020, the gem of an Art Deco studio apartment in East Melbourne that she stumbled upon was well out of her price range. Which made it so much harder when Tantri walked through the door and instantly knew this had to be her home. "I mean, it has a bloody curved wall and a tiny arched nook," she enthuses. "It's an Art Deco dream that ticked all the boxes aesthetics-wise – and all the practical stuff too."

Cut to many frantic conversations with the real estate agent, negotiating the price down, and the following November, Tantri picked up the keys to the apartment. "If I could stay here forever, I totally would," she exclaims.

The studio flat is small but perfectly formed, with big windows overlooking a small nook off the main room, where Tantri has installed a long table and bench, fitted specifically for the space and finished in black and white mosaic. As this is a rental, all of Tantri's improvements are temporary, but she thought this one out perfectly: the table doubles as a breakfast spot, a home office and an aperitif corner for sundowners. And given the flat's lack of storage space, the bench doubles as a hideaway for everything she doesn't have room to keep on display.

After a decade spent working as a hairdresser, Tantri was seeking a hands-on hobby that would allow her to express her creativity and help relieve stress and anxiety.

"I stumbled across clay. Soon after I was completely obsessed and I guess I just never stopped mucking around with the stuff! I enrolled myself into a couple of short courses and obsessively made ceramics in all of my spare time. Soon enough I had made some pieces I was really proud of and I decided to make a website (100 per cent thinking nothing would come of it!) and people ACTUALLY bought things!"

When the emails started flooding in, Tantri took a leap of faith and quit her job to pursue ceramics full time. Five years in, business is still going strong.

"I am pinching myself that in such a short time I have ended up in my dream studio space and have a little retail store, plus I get to teach people the thing that I love doing the most!"

Ceramicist

•

East Melbourne,
Victoria

111

"I am pinching myself that in such a short time I have ended up in my dream studio space and have a little retail store, plus I get to teach people the thing that I love doing the most!"

"I can be quite frantic as all of the people close to me know very well, so I find that making with my hands really grounds me and can centre me when things feel like they are a bit all over the place. I have realised over time that the less I make things with my hands, the more flustered I become in general. I would say, for me, making things with my hands is almost a method of active meditation."

Tantri has styled her interiors carefully, making intelligent use of the apartment's existing space. A cosy ochre-coloured couch slots perfectly along one wall, facing the bed – made with Bed Threads linen in oatmeal and terracotta – while a beloved chest of drawers, restored courtesy of a labour of DIY love many years ago, sits in one corner. Along the mantelpiece, Tantri has arranged some of her enviable ceramics collection.

She is always looking to add more ceramic pieces to her home. "But I truly don't think I have any space for anything else in my house currently," she admits. Though, she does have one thing on her wishlist: "I do really so badly want a Calacatta Viola marble coffee table from Harpers Project," she reveals. "A gal can dream, right? Maybe when I grow up I can have one."

KENDALL KNOX

*A relaxed beachside home with a mix
of antique, rustic and modern style.*

In Kendall Knox's Venice Beach pad, there are windows galore,
hardwood floors, a mint-green bathroom and views over the trees.
It is, in short, a perfect home base. It's also one that might never have
been Kendall's if it wasn't for a stroke of happy luck.

The furniture and interiors expert, who co-founded vintage home
decor business Olive Ateliers, had been searching for six months for
a new space with her partner, visiting house after house looking for the
perfect spot. "We knew we wanted a small yard, hardwood floors,
the craftsman charm Venice so often has to offer, and, most importantly,
somewhere within walking distance to the beach and restaurants
we love," she explains.

But it was taking a while. Then one day, walking to their car
after visiting a house that wasn't quite right, they spotted a For Lease
sign on their favourite Venice Beach street. "We peeked through
the window and I saw the classic built-ins in the dining room and
my heart skipped a beat envisaging all the ways I could decorate,"
she says. "After a little negotiation to get the rent to a less scary place,
we signed on the dotted line."

Since moving in, Kendall has filled the light-flooded space with
natural fibres, soft textiles, a mixture of different textures and antique
pieces sourced by the lifestyle brand she co-founded. The colour palette
is muted and cosy, leaning heavily on sage green, classic oatmeal and
white, with touches of turmeric.

"I'd say our space is a mix of monastic modern and European
farm style. Texture is king. I wanted to ensure we styled the space
with sustainability in mind, so plenty of vintage furniture and finds,
and natural, neutral fibres," she says.

Entrepreneur

•

Venice Beach,
Los Angeles,
United States

"I wanted to ensure we styled the space
with sustainability in mind, so [I've used]
plenty of vintage furniture and finds,
and natural, neutral fibres."

"I'm even guilty of using seasonal fruit and veg as decor — artichokes, lemons, limes, pears and figs right now. Their bumps and bruises add as much texture and charisma to the space as anything else."

The antique accents, such as Moroccan oil jars and vintage French vases, style well with Kendall's investment-piece furniture, including a sprawling lounge and an elm wood coffee table in the living room, and a cosy armchair in an airy corner of the main bedroom.

This bedroom is her favourite room. "I wanted a space with... tall ceilings to wake up to, nap, sip my morning coffee, enjoy the Sunday paper, work from, all of the above. If Ben let me, I'd potter around that bedroom all day long," she jokes. She's deliberately styled it minimally in order to maintain that air of relaxation and repose: aside from the bed, some stools, the chair and a big mirror, there's barely any other furniture in the space. "For us it felt important to minimise the clutter," Kendall explains. "You don't want to wake to chaos every day."

ZARA SEIDLER

Pastel hues, iconic Slim Aarons artwork,
sculptural furniture and retro lighting create
a timeless mid-century modern home.

Zara Seidler, co-founder of Australia's leading social-first news service, *The Daily Aus*, freely admits it was her partner who took care of most of the styling of her charming and peaceful mid-century apartment in Sydney's Bellevue Hill.

"Throughout this [interior design] process, we have recognised each other's strengths and weaknesses, and let's just say... I do news better than interior design," she laughs.

Starting your own media business, let alone in your early twenties, requires a clear vision, plenty of drive and a knack for innovation. And while the former political advisor spends most of her long (often 18-hour!) days, breaking down complex political and social issues to inform millennials, her home is serene, youthful and refined.

Zara holds a Bachelor of International and Global Studies from The University of Sydney, and her impressive, albeit short, career has seen her work as a research assistant in Washington DC, a Government Relations Officer, and an Electorate Officer.

She describes herself as loud, opinionated and addicted to explaining things, traits she encourages other young women to embrace in order to take risks and make themselves heard.

"I've honestly never considered myself as creative, and have therefore never thought about what my process looks like. In terms of innovating, which I believe is my form of creativity, I look to our audience of inspiring, engaged and loyal young people to inform what future innovation should look and feel like," she says.

Her light-flooded home leans towards a relaxed mid-century aesthetic with its stereo players, retro lighting and vintage chairs. Lashings of pastel hues enliven the apartment, from the iconic Slim Aarons poolside print that hangs above an aqua sideboard in the open-plan living area, to the pink clay and terracotta linen in the bedroom. Elegant details, such as leadlight windows and an ornate ceiling design, bring further character into the home and elevate it to a more sophisticated level.

Co-founder of
The Daily Aus

•

Bellevue Hill,
Sydney, NSW

119

"The afternoon light is beautiful,
and a Sunday arvo in bed with
a book is the best place to be."

"It was the first proper space I looked at," says Zara, "and I was drawn immediately to the outlook and light-flooded bedroom. I moved from living with my mum into this place, so it was a big move."

Her favourite spot at home to relax? "The bedroom. The afternoon light is beautiful, and a Sunday arvo in bed with a book is the best place to be."

ABBEY RICH

*The beautiful plant-filled home of a Melbourne
artist is surrounded by gumtrees.*

Artist Abbey Rich and their partner Sam found their Melbourne home almost by chance. The pair attended a birthday party for their friends' daughter and fell in love with the home it was held in. There was something about "the big windows", Abbey says, along with "the huge gumtrees you can see from streets away and the myriad of fruit trees." So, when the opportunity came up to make the place their own, the couple didn't hesitate.

Abbey is a painter and drawer who works on projects as large-scale as public murals and as small-scale as a tiny tattoo adorning the arm of one of their clients. Every job is different and requires a different creative process, they say. Big murals are planned out "methodically" while other personal works could come "tumbling out" after a period of feeling stuck. "It's an, at times, uncomfortable, but familiar process."

At home, there's a similarly collaborative and multi-purpose vibe. "The thing we think about most is how can we make it a functional space that can accommodate many friends, day in and day out," Abbey explains. There are plenty of chairs, lots of ceramics and a big table, all designed for maximum hosting with minimum fuss, while also being cosy enough when there's only Abbey and Sam in residence.

Most of the furniture in the couple's home was found, either in secondhand stores or elsewhere, or in the case of their kitchen bench, custom-made.

"My very sweet dad built us this incredible bench, entirely by hand (hand-sawn, hand-planed, etc). It is most definitely too tall for anyone under 6ft but works perfectly for us." says Abbey.

"I like collecting – whether it be a friend's work or little things we find on a trip," Abbey says. "So much stuff exists in the world, I think it's really easy to style well with secondhand things! All the furniture in our house, except our bed, was found. Even our two big rugs were found in hard rubbish right on our street."

Artist

•

Pascoe Vale South,
Melbourne, Victoria

123

Their most treasured items, though, are artworks by their favourite creatives including Julia Trybala, Felix Atkinson and Joy Yamusangie. Those, along with their photo album, represent Abbey's most beloved possessions. "I've made a really conscious effort to regularly print out photos from trips and just our everyday life," they say. "I look at it almost weekly."

Abbey's advice when decorating a home? "Just go with what you feel."

"So much stuff exists in the world,
I think it's really easy to style well
with secondhand things!"

THE PERFECT BEDROOM

*Some of our favourite creatives share
their top tips for a well-styled sleep space.*

The primary bedroom is the space in the home where
you can completely relax and curl up, and express your
personal style. It's where you start and end your day,
and how well it is designed can impact both your
physical and mental wellbeing.

But given it is the most private room in the home
and is typically on show less often, it can be easy
to neglect its aesthetic.

There are plenty of places to seek inspiration for
decorating your bedroom, but as far as getting advice,
who better to ask than creative people who have a keen
eye for detail and dedicate their lives to the arts?

TALI ROTH, INTERIOR DESIGNER

"Try and keep symmetry for a sense of space and opulence; i.e. if you can have two side tables and two lamps or sconces then do."

ASHLEIGH HOLMES, ARTIST

"Buy once and buy well. Select pieces that you feel you'll keep for a lifetime. Timeless and quality is my view on styling. I like neutral but I also feel it's important to have colour in our life as it hands us a sensory emotion."

JORDAN FERNEY, ENTREPRENEUR

"Create systems so that it can stay nice and serene. For example, have a place for dirty clothes so even when you are busy, your room can feel calm. Fill it with art and flowers and things that make you happy."

SIMONE HAAG, INTERIOR DESIGNER

"A well-styled bedroom for me means everything has to serve a purpose. You don't just have cushions for cushions' sake. The cushion is there for comfort so you can work on your laptop, read a book or snuggle with family. A bed is all well and good, but you have to be able to sit in it and enjoy the room it's in. You need to make your bedroom a place that evokes cosiness and warmth."

HANNAH SINDORF, JEWELLER

"Having a space that's a reflection of you and what you love is my best advice. It's not about what's trendy, it's about having a collection of objects that pull you in and bring you joy. That's what will ultimately make a space feel like home."

SARAH PICKERSGILL-BROWN, EDITORIAL STYLIST

"I love using natural fibres like linen on the beds and wooden furniture so the overall feeling is relaxed and warm. I include a variety of heights and textures to create interest. Sheer curtains filter the natural light beautifully and create a dreamy atmosphere. These look best when hung floor to ceiling to accentuate height."

JESSICA BELLEF, INTERIOR STYLIST

"Always add more books, more art, and more lamps, but leave some breathing space. Negative space is powerful and can help create a calm room that gives you the space to let happiness and good thoughts in."

DANIEL BODDAM, ARCHITECT

"I like the mantra less is more. Few, but edited, pieces that have breathing space. A bedroom should be a restful atmosphere, so working with complementary colours and natural materials works well. I tend to favour layered monochromatic and neutral colours and rely on art for pops of colour."

JAZ MEIER, ARTIST

"For me personally it needs to be warm and inviting. I also think plants are essential in every room. Bringing a bit of life and nature indoors changes the whole dynamic of a room to me."

LYNDA GARDENER, INTERIOR DESIGNER

"Lots of layers, textures, keeping to a colour palette that suits not just the room but the entire home. The beds are so important to me: colour, texture, layers. Pure linen always. A throw or two and roughly styled scatter cushions, nothing over-styled, quite relaxed and loose."

FIRST
HOMES

After months (sometimes years) of searching,
turning the key in your own front door is one
of life's most exciting moments. Home-cooking
expert Jessica Nguyen turned her first home into
an entertainer's paradise, while artist Ashleigh
Holmes transformed an apartment on Sydney's
Northern Beaches into a total zen den.

ALI WHITTLE

*This historic home has been reinvented with
pops of pastels and brightly hued trinkets.*

As is the story with most artistic types, Ali Whittle knew from an early
age that she would enter into a creative field professionally. As someone
who loves writing, pop culture and the idea of a fast-paced working
environment, she was quick to decide at 14 that she wanted to work in
magazines. Fast forward to now and Ali has lived her dream: after stints
on various fashion and mainstream titles including *WHO Magazine*,
she is currently working as a digital content creator and influencer.

Ali and her architect husband Angus had been looking to buy for
nearly a year when they stumbled across their now home in 2021.
"As soon as I walked in I had a very good feeling. It felt familiar and
so special. The location is perfect. It feels like we live in a rainforest
in the middle of nowhere, but we're so close to everything. By the
following week our offer was accepted and it was ours. We couldn't
believe it. We still feel so lucky and we love everything about it. It keeps
getting better and better."

Ali is drawn to colour and this is widely reflected in her
decor choices. The interior's overall look is fun and kaleidoscopic,
yet perfectly sophisticated. "I love colour, beautiful trinkets, making
my space special and unique," she says.

A terracotta-toned rug anchors the living area which features chic
Sarah Ellison seating, vibrant Dowel Jones side tables, and a playful
artwork by Manyjilyjarra artist Doreen Chapman. The main bedroom
upstairs is sunny and bright thanks to the high ceilings, limoncello
linen, and a charming balcony that floods the space with natural light.

Perhaps the most striking area of the home, however, is the
kitchen where the joinery has been swathed in a deep seafoam green
and is complemented by timber countertops. "We spend a lot more
time cooking in this kitchen than in our previous places, as it's a really
comfortable, nice space to prepare food in. It gets amazing morning
light too," she shares.

Digital content
creator
+
Influencer

•

Edgecliff,
Sydney, NSW

With renovation plans in the works and special decor pieces they'd like to add, they are in no rush: "It's nice to just live in the space and really work out what's needed, but it's also very fun to plan and create a vision."

"We're going to build banquette seating in our dining area as well as a new pendant light for that area. Some more art, new beds, wall sconces... the list goes on. I think I'll be forever looking, adding and tweaking because it's what I love to do," she says.

"I love colour, beautiful trinkets, making my space special and unique."

134

ASHLEIGH HOLMES

*This renovated beachside apartment
adopts a muted palette with
a mix of old and new pieces.*

Ashleigh Holmes renovated her home on Sydney's Northern Beaches
to create a serene living space she can retreat to with her partner
Jake. Located in the beachside suburb of Curl Curl, the apartment was
transformed with the help of the painter's friend, Mariah Madder
of Folk Studio, and is imbued with a minimal, contemporary Japanese
sensibility, warmed up with wabi-sabi touches.

"My studio is chaotic at times and usually messy, so I like
to come home to a space that's clean," she says. Her home's muted
colour palette also taps into the hues of her favourite landscapes, with
warm neutrals and varying shades punctuating the otherwise white
scheme. "I'm inspired by the way that being in nature makes us feel, why
it has such a calming effect on us and what colour combinations I can
learn from the natural landscape." Ashleigh says she also draws from
Japanese design: "I'm in awe of their craftsmanship and eye for the finer
details of objects." Rustic timber beams salvaged from an old wharf were
placed above the sheer curtains in the living room and main bedroom,
bringing a wabi-sabi touch.

The curved walnut table and walnut wine rack in the dining
space were handmade by Ashleigh's brother and extend the handcrafted
motif. To keep things cohesive and in keeping with the Japanese-
inspired aesthetic, walnut timber was also used in the kitchen and
bathroom joinery. The bathroom features green tiles in a vertical
subway pattern on both the floors and walls for a look that's calming
and stylish.

Ashleigh says timeless and quality is her view when it comes
to styling. "Buy once and buy well. Select pieces that you feel you'd
keep for a lifetime," she says. "I like neutrals but I also feel it's important
to have colour in our life as it hands us a sensory emotion."

Colour also comes via Ashleigh's own artworks. In her practice,
she draws on colour psychology and her environment to create her
ever-evolving abstract paintings. These large-scale works, dotted
around her house, have made her a finalist in the Mosman Art Prize,
in the Lloyd Rees Memorial Youth Art Award and the Premio Combat
Prize, and have seen her selected as the resident artist for the Harbord
Hotel in Sydney.

Artist
+
Founder
of Hake House

•

Curl Curl,
Sydney, NSW

137

"I'm inspired by the way that being in nature makes us feel, why it has such a calming effect on us and what colour combinations I can learn from the natural landscape."

FATUMA NDENZAKO

*Colourful, eye-catching and full of treasures,
this fashion designer's family home is relaxed yet bold.*

Fatuma Ndenzako can thank her little boy for her beautiful home. The co-founder and designer of the Melbourne-based Collective Closets conscious fashion brand had spent months looking for a new house with her husband, but nothing was right. Then, one afternoon, they "accidentally arrived at the open house", she recalls. As the family did a circuit through the building, their son yelled, "This is perfect, I love this, Mum," Fatuma says. "With an endorsement like that, we knew we had found our home," she adds.

That was a few years ago, and the family of three are well-settled into their new space. Renovations were fairly minimal when they first moved: a lick of white paint on the walls – "I couldn't live with cream walls," she jokes – and new light fittings in the kitchen and living areas.

Colourful and eye-catching yet still relaxed, Fatuma's home is full of pieces that she and her husband have owned for years, such as their wooden dining table, purchased 11 years ago. Over time, Fatuma has added key pieces of decor to their home too, like the day bed - which they are going to re-upholster in green velvet - that she admits has long been a dream of hers to own.

Fatuma will be the first to admit she doesn't really have a process when it comes to styling her space. "I just buy what I love," she explains, "and sometimes it works and sometimes it doesn't. I am still learning the perfect balance." But it's true, there's a lot of love in this home, from the living areas full of many collected treasures to the warm tones of her peaceful bedroom. "I believe your bedroom is where your soul rests," she advises, "so you don't want to fill it up with too much clutter. I think it's nice to have a plant, too."

Bright, patterned works throughout the home are nods to the statement-making styles she creates for her brand. Co-founded with her sister Laurinda, the pair produce apparel that pays homage to their African roots while also referencing the trends on the streets of Melbourne. It's this unique style that has found them a community of followers, both online and through their former store at Melbourne's iconic Queen Victoria Market.

Fashion designer

•

Coburg,
Melbourne, Victoria

143

"I've always given my all to my work. I got my first job when I was 14 and I've worked ever since," she says. "I have been extremely lucky to have worked for some great businesses who always supported me on my Collective Closets journey. Every role has taught me and helped me develop the skills that I'm using now. My philosophy is to go deep into what you do, but when you lose the happiness or the challenge, keep moving."

144

"I just buy what I love...
sometimes it works and
sometimes it doesn't."

JESSICA NGUYEN

*This eclectic and stylish home
is an entertainer's paradise.*

Jessica Nguyen's dining room is the heart of the house. Are you
surprised? The Melbourne-based home chef loves to entertain and
her many thousands of followers adore her easygoing and carefree
attitude to cooking. Of course she was going to have a big dining room,
complete with a bar station displaying Campari, gin and sweet red
vermouth – everything you need to make a killer negroni. And of course
the dining room, with its table for six and its big pools of warm light,
would be the room she spends the most time in.

It's easy to think, given how fervent her Instagram following is and
how perfectly put together her recipes are, that Jessica has been doing
this forever. But the pivot to cooking content only happened when
she was made redundant from her marketing and PR job at the start
of 2020. Faced with self-isolation and a long stretch of time spent
at home, Jessica turned to food as a salve.

She has always loved cooking, and often shared kitchen content
on her socials, but never professionally or in earnest. But when her recipes
really started resonating with readers, she realised she had stumbled
upon a new, and delicious, career.

"I'm a firm believer that things happen for a reason and
sometimes beautiful things fall apart for better things to come
together," explains Jessica. "My journey of how I landed in this fairly
new career is exactly that."

Jessica cooks all of her recipes in the kitchen of her 110-year-old
Edwardian-style Melbourne home, which she shares with her husband
and their two dogs. From the second she set foot in the kitchen, with
its five-burner Italian oven, Jessica knew that this house was The
One. That feeling only intensified when she learned that the previous
owners were importers of Italian wine and ran food tours in Italy,
the home of some of her favourite dishes. "When we met [them]
to get the keys, what was meant to be a quick meeting turned into
at least six bottles of wine on the decking on a Sunday afternoon,"
she recalls. "This house was just meant to be."

Cook
+
Creative

•

Armadale,
Melbourne, Victoria

"Buy vintage as much as you can.
It's more sustainable, generally cheaper
and adds more character to your home."

Just like her taste in recipes, the style in Jessica's home is eclectic. "I style my interiors the same way I create recipes; never stick to one cuisine, theme, style or era because life is too short to just do one thing. That being said, just like I do tend to lean towards Italian and Asian recipes, I do love anything that is vintage from the Art Deco, mid century and Hollywood Regency periods. Finally, just like the perfect home or recipe, it still has to be functional/delicious!"

Not surprising for an entertainer, her favourite room in the house is the open-plan living and dining area: "I love our open living and dining room that looks out to our garden. It's the cosiest part of the house, I spend the most time in these two areas, it's the most open, biggest room, has the best light during the day and has the best memories of people and parties we've hosted and enjoyed in this space."

And her styling tips for a chic sleeping space? "I like to keep this space cool, calm and collected with soothing and mainly blue tones. However, the rest of my house where I live during the day is bright, more fun and eclectic, but still functional. Also buy vintage as much as you can. It's more sustainable, generally cheaper, and adds more character to your home."

AMANDA HINKELMANN

The First Nations artist celebrates her heritage via intricate and unique paintings throughout her home.

First Nations art is deeply meaningful, celebrating the strong spiritual connection Indigenous Australians have to family, community and Country. For Wiradjuri artist Amanda Hinkelmann, creating art allows her to pay homage to her heritage. "I work respectfully to promote my culture, telling stories through my art," she says. "My hope is that each day more and more people see how beautiful and deep our culture is, so we can move forward together as a nation."

After completing a primary education degree at university, Amanda taught as a school teacher for 14 years before spending another year working as a school principal. In 2019 she decided to dedicate her time to pursuing art as a full-time career. "I love creating every day and find that when I allow myself time to be creative I am completely myself," she says.

Each of her special artworks embraces a dot painting style and incorporates up to 10 layers of acrylic paint. Stamped in vivid colours and intricate patterns, these contemporary works offer a unique and meaningful display in a home and are well suited to a wide range of interior-design styles. Many of Amanda's artworks hang on the walls of her home in Wagga Wagga, a regional city in New South Wales, four hours south-west of Sydney. They bring life, history and beauty to the abode, which she shares with her husband and children. The home also contains her art studio which was created by converting the second living room. "I have completely ruined the space with paint, but I must admit, it is definitely my happy place and you'll find me there every day!" she says.

"We moved in when our house was new, working with the builder to adjust the floor plan and interior finishes. We have changed the flooring in the living spaces for easier cleaning, but besides that, we haven't adjusted much. We have not long ago put a pool in and are in the process of landscaping our backyard. My husband is hoping for a tropical paradise in the middle of Wagga!" she says.

Artist

•

Wagga Wagga,
NSW

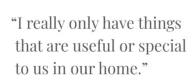

"I really only have things
that are useful or special
to us in our home."

The decor choices in the home have been carefully selected to reflect her artworks. This is perhaps most successfully achieved in the primary bedroom where warm tones of terracotta, peach and rosewater beautifully complement the aerial landscape painting that hangs above the bed.

Her tip for a harmonious home is to banish clutter. "Those who know me know that I don't do clutter!" she says. "I can't stand having 'things' around me for the sake of it, so I am forever getting rid of stuff. I really only have things that are useful or special to us in our home. It makes for a cleaner, calmer space and there is less to have to pick up. My nan used to tell me, 'A place for everything, and everything in its place'. I live by this! As far as styling goes, I love warm tones, texture, and handmade. You can't beat it."

MADELEINE HOY

*A change of pace and a chronic illness
translated into a joyful new path and a gorgeous
Art Deco home for this designer.*

From an early age, Madeleine Hoy knew she wanted to explore
her creativity and run her own design business one day. "I think
this way of thinking was inspired by my dad who had some very
special restaurants in his career. I wanted to have a similar experience
of developing a concept and sharing it with people," she explains.

After studying set and costume design at NIDA, Madeleine moved
onto work in the events industry where she was able to collaborate
with many high-profile brands and gain an insight into how design
is explored through various lenses. It also strengthened her longing
to create something of her very own.

Enter Nonna's Grocer, Madeleine's studio and concept shop,
where she designs and creates joyfully bright and bold handmade
candles in the shapes of fruits and vegetables, all in such realistic detail
they could be edible. Other design objects are also in the works.

The idea for Nonna's Grocer was inspired by a story her father told
her about the fruit shop her great grandfather owned in Daylesford,
Victoria, in the 1930s. After struggling with a debilitating chronic illness
Madeleine took some time away from her everyday job to rest, which
is when she began to tinker with the idea to make fruit-shaped candles.

"Being a designer and coping with a health issue has certainly been
the trickiest part of my career thus far, particularly with the deadline
pressure that is embedded in the creative industry," says Madeleine.
"I have struggled through the hardest part though, which is re-calibrating
how I work and factoring in time for myself when I am not well. But it has
taught me that health comes first and that when you are open and honest
about your situation, people are genuinely accommodating and kind,"
she says.

Moving from Sydney "for a change of pace" marks another
change in Madeleine's life that has seen her settle in a gorgeous,
simply renovated 1950s home in Wollongong.

"It was the Art Deco architecture and gorgeous wild garden
that caught our eye. It had a lovely charm about it, we had to have it,"
she says. "We have had the easy task of just moving our furniture in,
and enjoying the home and the beautiful details in all its glory."

Designer
+
Founder of
Nonna's Grocer

•

Wollongong,
NSW

A warm and welcoming feeling permeates the light-filled home, rich with wooden details and neutral tones. A stunning highlight is the dining room with large decorative curved windows, where light streams over the large table draped in mustard linen and decorated with fresh posies and Madeleine's candles.

"There is something about a curved window that is always so inviting, and we love having meals there with our garden as the backdrop," she says.

In the bedroom, muted pastel hues continue, a playful print by Sydney artist Madeline Jovicic carries on the fruit theme and hangs over a bed made with turmeric and pink linens.

Madeleine advises "collecting things you love" to add when styling your home. "Carry the light *and* heavy things back from your travels if you think you will love them forever," she says.

"Carry the light *and* heavy things back from your travels if you think you will love them forever."

LEIGH
CAMPBELL

*This media maven's apartment
is the definition of luxe minimalism.*

Once upon a time, Leigh Campbell thought she might work in the
world of interiors, completing a course at The Whitehouse Institute.
But somewhere along the way she "fell into media" and the interiors
plan was left by the wayside. It was, Leigh says, "a happy mistake".
Since then, she has worked in the world of magazines and online
media at major mastheads including *Cosmopolitan*, *Huffington Post* and
Mamamia, as well as running beauty podcast and newsletter *You Beauty*,
and pregnancy and postpartum body product brand, Brillo Beauty.

But Leigh's interiors knowledge was useful when it came
to renovating her three-bedroom flat in Sydney's Eastern Suburbs.
A heavily pregnant Leigh and her husband had been searching for six
months when they took a look at a place they'd seen online. Though
she describes their decision to buy the apartment after one viewing
as a combination of "desperation and intense nesting urges", she says
the flat is another happy mistake. A few renovations later, including
a new kitchen and a bathroom with a big tub for soaking in, the young
family are well settled in their new digs.

Leigh's design process is simple and stress-free, a combination
of all the things she has loved over the years brought together harmoniously
in her home. Tying it all together is a luxe and lush minimalism, all
neutral colours and plush soft furnishings. "I like to keep things neutral,
bright colours feel like screaming in my head," Leigh jokes. "I have a toddler,
though, so there are plenty of primary coloured toys strewn around."

When the couple first moved in, Leigh had big wardrobes installed
in the bedrooms but her biggest piece of advice is to invest in a good-
quality bed. "You lay there for a third of your life – though less with
a baby – so it's cash well spent," she says. "Our bed feels like a hotel
bed, big and tall. I don't like beds too close to the ground, they feel
unfinished." And her tip for a well-styled bedroom? "Make a focal point
for above the bed. We have a shelf with two artworks that I always get
comments on, and some beautiful candles. I wanted something slightly
different than just one big print, which is pretty predictable."

Beauty
editor
+
Co-founder
of Brillo Beauty

•

Randwick,
Sydney, NSW

"Our bed feels like a hotel bed, big and tall.
I don't like beds too close to the ground;
they feel unfinished."

AFFORDABLE ART

*A beginner's guide to collecting
art on a budget.*

No longer a hobby reserved for the wealthy, art collecting
has become affordable, accessible and a deeply satisfying
way to spend your hard-earned cash.

Whether you're looking to create the perfect gallery
wall in your home, or you've just discovered an amazing
new artist you'd love to invest in, it's worth putting some
time and thought into how you're going to build your
art collection.

Dipping a toe into the art world can be famously
intimidating but it doesn't have to be daunting or
overwhelming. Here are some tips for how to start
a collection on a tighter budget.

1. DO YOUR HOMEWORK

Collecting art is a game of delayed gratification. It can be hard to resist the urge to build a complete collection straight away, but your bank account and your eyes will be better off if you take the time to research, plan and budget. It's better to have blank walls than a house full of impulse buys.

While you don't need to have a degree in art history to dive in, doing your research is essential. Try to familiarise yourself with the basics (mediums, styles, artistic eras) to understand which art you like, love and can't bear to look at for more than a few seconds.

Art is inherently social, so go to galleries, art fairs, exhibition openings, scroll through social media, talk to artists you like, and chat with gallery owners or staff about the artists they represent and the pieces on display. Look into the exhibition history of artists you enjoy, or prizes they have won. This is how you'll find unique pieces that have had an impact.

2. CRUNCH THE NUMBERS

Buying art can quickly become addictive, and if you jump in too quickly, you run the risk of spending a chunk of money on something you'll get sick of in six months. Decide how often you want to add to your collection and set aside money each month. If you aim for a yearly art budget of $500 upwards, in 10 years you will have 10 amazing pieces with a great story.

Keep in mind that buying directly from artists or online galleries can be cheaper as there are no overheads involved. High-end galleries usually charge more than up-and-comers, and previously owned works being sold through an auction will also usually be more expensive. Don't forget to factor in insurance, shipping and framing.

3. BUY WHAT YOU LOVE

Don't buy what you can live with: buy what you can't live without. Buying art you love will always be a good investment. Start small, whether that's literally smaller pieces, lesser-known artists or smaller galleries, and build from there.

Don't disregard photographs, drawings, limited editions, sculptures, and art books. These can all be cheaper than paintings and make your collection an interesting and eclectic one. Buying original artwork rather than a print will also add more value.

RENOVATIONS & BUILDS

From Amanda Callan's refurbished church house
to Pandora Sykes' charming Victorian terrace,
these inspiring homes have been totally transformed
by their creative owners. While renovating can
be more than difficult, these jaw-dropping spaces
prove it's well worth the effort, especially when
the end results turn out like these...

PANDORA SYKES

*This playful Victorian terrace is the work of
an inquisitive and creative wordsmith.*

As someone who is naturally interested in the way people live, what they read, watch and talk about, it makes sense that Pandora Sykes has always known she wanted to be a journalist. Beginning her career as a fashion journalism intern, the UK-born creative is now renowned for her brilliant social commentary and impressive portfolio of work that includes contributions to esteemed titles such as *The Guardian*, *The Sunday Times, ELLE, GQ, Grazia* and *Vogue,* several popular podcasts and her *Sunday Times* bestselling book, *How Do We Know We're Doing It Right?*, a collection of essays that explore her musings on modern life.

Pandora evidently has a way with words, but she also has an eye for interior design, which shows throughout her beautiful London terrace home. Boasting whimsy and sophistication, it's a study in how to use colour, pattern and eclectic decor to create a home truly reflective of your personal style.

From the turmeric-toned living room to the pink-hued main bedroom, her Victorian terrace is swathed in lashings of colour, executed in a way that feels harmonious from room to room.

"I like colour and I like decoration but there's also a restraint, I think, because I don't like rooms to look like rainbows and I hate (hate!) clutter," Pandora explains.

There is also a definite playfulness to the home's design. Patterned wallpaper and soft furnishings, ornate decor and various styles of artwork culminate to create a cosy yet chic scheme that looks expertly put together.

"I also don't mind things looking a bit 'bad taste' - I have leopard print curtains, so that's obvious - and I love vintage and antiques," Pandora says. From the eclectic mix of furniture to the plethora of accessories, the home's design feels masterfully thought out and steeped in love. "A house is a living thing and I like it to feel like a dynamic space," she says of the ongoing design process.

Journalist
+
Author

•

London,
United Kingdom

175

"A house is a living thing and I like
 it to feel like a dynamic space."

GINA LASKER

This florist's home-meets-workspace
is blooming with colour and charm.

Floral arrangements have a unique ability to completely transform the look and feel of a space. They bring a natural element indoors and can lift our mood with their beauty. Founder of Melbourne-based floral studio Georgie Boy, Gina Lasker's exquisite creations not only bring pure joy to recipients but also help elevate a home, event space or restaurant, tenfold.

Gina's charming home conveniently sits above her workspace. It's peppered with a mix of contemporary and mid-century furniture and decor, and of course, an ever-changing array of alluring blooms.

"There wasn't a plan for the interiors, it really just happened over time," she says. "It's a balance of old and new pieces that we will no doubt have forever".

From the kitchen island to the bedroom walls, the home is clad in light timber that exudes an organic and relaxed look. No stranger to colour, Gina has embraced a neutral base with lashings of various hues throughout her home. The cosy bedroom nook celebrates warm tones of turmeric and oatmeal encased in light timber walls for a cocooning effect.

"Dan [my partner] and I love wood and colour. Everything was brought into the space for the space or built by Dan to fit the space. We still want more art on the walls, but again... everything in good time!" she says.

Like any artistic field that produces a beautiful end result, floristry requires focus and can be intense and fast-paced. Gina strives to find the balance between life and work, however difficult it can often be.

She takes a relaxed approach to creating her sanctuary at home: "It's still heaven on earth to me even with the parts that aren't finished. Most days I wake up, look out the windows and think about how lucky we are to have this space."

Gina's main tip for a beautiful bedroom and home is staying true to your personal style.

"For me with a bedroom, less is more. I like where I sleep to have as little in it as possible but this means you can be bold with the bed linen. Dan in particular loves some colour on the bed, while I like to mix it up from neutral to colourful. Styling is so personal. What you surround yourself with has a huge impact on how you feel, so as long as it works for you, you're doing it right."

Florist

•

Northcote,
Melbourne, Victoria

181

"Most days I wake up, look out the
windows and think about how lucky
we are to have this space."

ANNIE PORTELLI

Welcome inside this beautifully renovated 1950s apartment.

Art
director

•

North Melbourne,
Victoria

First things first, let's talk about those terrazzo countertops. The centrepieces of art director Annie Portelli's kitchen and bathroom are two huge slabs of chunky, stone-studded terrazzo. The "blessed" stone benches are her favourite thing in the North Melbourne apartment she has owned for the past six years. "My conversation starter," Annie exclaims. "They are my pride and joy."

But they almost didn't happen. After purchasing the flat, situated in Melbourne's renowned 1959 apartment complex 'Hotham Gardens', built with windows on each side and flooded with light, Annie went through five months of purely aesthetic renovations in order to achieve her interior "vision". The goal was to bring the place together into one unified design, creating a space that felt warm, inviting and lived-in.

That's where the terrazzo came in: a benchtop that would run around the curve of the kitchen and in the bathroom, rippled through with big shards of stones in shades of mossy green and terracotta. Because her parents were helping with the renovation, "both physically and financially," Annie pitched the idea to them and was met with rolled eyes and the advice to keep it simple.

"They were right to say that," Annie muses. "I pretty quickly gave up on the terrazzo dream and started to seek out other options. A couple of weeks later, my dad emailed me at 3:15am exclaiming 'We can do this!' To which I then rolled my eyes." But they did it – "Well, he did it," she jokes. "Now it's the hero of the house."

In her day job as art director for *The Design Files*, Annie harnesses the ideas and vision of the brand for events, photoshoots and more. "*The Design Files* has a specific 'feel' to it, and it's my job to maintain and push that feel each time something new goes out into the world.

"In most cases with any of these projects or events that we have, I start with a moodboard and a visual direction. This is often done well before any of the serious stuff, like the timeline or the event location. But I like to do this really early on and present it to the team to get them all excited. We're all so visual, so this part of the process is quite important for all of us – it makes it feel like it's a 'real thing'."

It's not just the terrazzo that makes Annie's apartment a truly special space. It might be small, but the interiors are perfectly formed, with furniture custom built to fit into the space, such as the dining table made by Thomas Lentini, and sentimental artwork and objects styled in every corner. No wonder she has lived here for six years: it's tranquil and soothing. The kind of place you want to come home to every day.

"I like to keep the furnishings and objects textural, but tonal," Annie says. "When you look at the apartment as a whole, there are some subtle pops of colour but generally everything is timber, tan or grey. This somehow allows the space to feel light in weight, and calm. The perfect living environment for me."

"I like to keep the furnishings and objects textural, but tonal."

MAFALDA VASCONCELOS

*It's all about light and colour in this
Melbourne artist's sanctuary.*

Around three years ago, Mafalda Vasconcelos and her partner started
looking for a house. The artist, who originally hails from Mozambique
and is now based in Melbourne, estimates the couple looked at about
50 different places without any luck. Then, they stumbled upon this
little jewel, a '70s-era build with "a backyard, front garden, deck, large
windows and a lot of light". In the living area, a vaulted ceiling gave
the whole space a sense of ceremony. The couple were sold. "This is not
our dream home," Mafalda adds, "but it is an amazing and cosy home
to start."

Since then, the artist has been slowly renovating the building.
Because her art practice is so grounded in colour – she trained first
in fashion design but now paints portraits and nude studies of women
– Mafalda wanted her home to be more of a tranquil sanctuary. Some
small changes included painting the walls and ceiling white, and paring
back any excess furniture. "Because I work creating 'things', I wanted
the house to be quite minimal in terms of furniture," Mafalda explains.
"I find that open spaces with fewer pieces make me and my partner
appreciate the house a lot more."

"I have always been very creative and growing up the youngest
child and an introvert, I found entertainment and refuge in making
things. I used to sell my creations to my family and friends or even
at small markets," she says.

"Nowadays, making is a form of prayer or meditation. I am
not religious; however, I am very spiritual and feel lucky to be able
to connect to that part of myself through the act of 'making'. There
are quite a few 'makers' in my family too. So, the act of making is
essential to my personality and it is how I connect with my identity."

Artist

•

Richmond,
Melbourne, Victoria

Every design detail in Mafalda's house makes a statement, from the couple's charcoal grey sofa to their collection of ritual objects and masks, artisanal pieces – such as a handmade wooden banana bowl from a Mozambique maker – vintage books and sculptures. "These objects are also very colourful because we love colour," Mafalda says – no wonder she's opted for rich ruby, pink clay and terracotta linen. White walls, lots of light and plain wooden floorboards serve as the perfect backdrop for all these treasured items to really sing.

"Surround yourself with objects that you love and that remind you of something valuable to you," she advises anyone looking to decorate their home. "Seek out family photos, artworks by creatives that inspire you, books that stimulate your mind and take you on imaginary journeys. Outside of yourself, your home should be the closest expression of who you are and where you've been," she says.

And her advice about pursuing your passion? "Just go for it and never expect others to do the work for you. If there is a will, there is a way. Believe in yourself and never give up on your purpose. I wish I had started earlier, and I wish I had faith in myself when I was younger."

"Just go for it and never expect others
to do the work for you. If there is a will,
there is a way."

JESSICA CHOI

The Melbourne-based ceramicist turned
a rundown terrace into a calming oasis.

Jessica Choi never thought her hobby would turn into her main source of income when she enrolled in a community pottery course in 2016. The then-production coordinator simply saw ceramics as a creative way to pass the time.

Then during lockdown in 2020, the Melbourne-based creative started to take her ceramics more seriously, and decided to take a leap of faith by selling her pieces. While she said she felt embarrassed after receiving no sales in the first two weeks, she persisted and followed her intuition, which she admits has been the best decision she's ever made.

Jessica now pursues her craft full-time with her thriving business Eun Ceramics. This is where she gets to channel her creative energy every day – a process she describes as therapeutic, exciting and rewarding. Inspired by the fluidity of clay, her soft, earthy-toned pieces are equal parts delicate and strong; fluid and bold, and it's these same traits you can see echoed throughout her renovated Melbourne home.

In addition to starting her business in 2020, Jessica and her husband were also house-hunting for their dream period-style home. They stumbled across a terrace within their budget; however, there was one problem – it was rundown to the point of being "derelict" and needed a heavy makeover. But the couple decided to go for it and now, five months of renovations later, they boast a beautiful home.

Since moving in, the couple have ripped out and rebuilt the kitchen and bathroom – a process Jessica documents on her addictive TikTok account. They've decorated the space minimally, opting for a clean colour palette of whites and oatmeals, with pops of greenery and rust. While it looks uniform at first glance, look closely and you'll see each room has been cleverly designed with a different theme: one playful, one classic and one minimal. Jessica didn't want to settle on one specific style, so it was her way of adding a wealth of character and warmth to her home.

Ceramicist

•

Ascot Vale,
Melbourne, Victoria

The minimal bedroom fitted with Bed Threads sheets in stripe and white gives the space a cloud-like, relaxing feel. In the lounge room, the emerald velvet rug, mid-century black chairs and modern oatmeal coffee table cohesively work together to create a place perfect for entertaining guests. The bathroom – her favourite room in the home – is fitted with a show-stopping free-standing bathtub. And to harmonise everything, her bold ceramics are sprinkled throughout.

"Although everything is still a bit of a work-in-progress, it's been incredibly enjoyable seeing my vision come to life," Jessica says.

"Although everything is still a bit of a work-in-progress, it's been incredibly enjoyable seeing my vision come to life."

BREE JOHNSON

*This tranquil, inner-city oasis
boasts natural tones, sleek design
and a breezy main bedroom.*

You'd be hard-pressed to find a beauty lover who isn't familiar with Australian skincare brand, frank body. Adored for its irreverent packaging, naturally derived ingredients and, of course, those addictive coffee scrubs, the brand is the brainchild of five friends whose mission was to make clean skincare fun. Launched in 2013, co-founder Bree Johnson has been instrumental in transforming this once small business into the global beauty empire it is today.

Growing up, Bree had never considered starting her own business. She studied journalism at university and kickstarted her career as an editorial assistant for *Broadsheet*. It was here that she was inspired by founder Nick Shelton's success in creating a company from the ground up, and it opened her eyes to what an entrepreneurial career could look like. "I quickly realised I didn't want to work for an entrepreneur," she shares. "I wanted to be one."

This idea led Bree to utilise her copywriting background and create branding agency Willow & Blake to help launch and build brands and their campaigns. Two years later, frank body was born.

Bree's home embraces a similar design ethos to frank body, boasting a sleek, clean aesthetic and natural tones. Bree and her husband chose a textural palette of materials including warm concrete, steel, light timber and linen, all of which not only look great but are sturdy, too – perfect for a growing family. "Our house is made to be lived in so we needed pieces that can withstand a toddler climbing over them with peanut-butter hands," she says.

The open-plan kitchen and dining area spills out onto a quaint, vine-filled courtyard area via large bifold doors. This section of the home is ideal for entertaining and allows natural light and air to enter the interior living spaces. "For furniture we chose quality, timeless pieces with a focus on comfort and functionality," she says. The star of the show here is undeniably the deep turquoise Togo couch that sits within the living area and is the perfect example of comfort meets style.

Co-founder
of frank body

•

Richmond,
Melbourne, Victoria

"Richmond gets busy so we wanted our home to feel calm," Bree says. "Like a little inner-city oasis."

"The idea is that the front rooms are a modern interpretation of the original period home and the new renovation is modern Australian," she says. Soothing blue and green hues prevail in each room, creating harmony between spaces and an overall peaceful aesthetic. The breezy main bedroom utilises mineral and sage linen to create a tranquil atmosphere and is paired perfectly with the coastal photograph that hangs above the bed. Bree's favourite room in the house is her study "because it's a space that's just for me."

"Our house is made to be lived in so we needed pieces that can withstand a toddler climbing over them with peanut-butter hands."

AMANDA CALLAN

AMANDA CALLAN

AMANDA CALLAN

*An old church in regional New South Wales
transformed beautifully into a dream family home.*

When Amanda Callan and her partner Andrew Morris discovered an old church in the small town of Billinudgel in northern New South Wales, they instantly knew the empty hall was going to become their dream family home. "When we first drove up and saw the For Sale sign with a mobile number I felt sick in my stomach because I knew it was ours," Amanda recalls.

After much-needed renovations – raising the church from the ground to protect it from flooding, adding a deck, a mezzanine, more bathrooms and a bedroom space – the old church was transformed into a home for their family of six. "It was just an empty hall with a tiny bathroom when we moved in, no kitchen, no bedrooms, full of mosquitoes," says Amanda. The new design kept the majority of the church's interior open with a sprawling living, kitchen and dining area, and sections partitioned off for bedrooms for their four young sons. "We are very much deep in the family zone at the moment," Amanda says.

It's here, in the open-plan kitchen and living area, that Amanda and Andrew create products for their business, Church Farm General Store. Handmade soaps, rich with essential oils, are on offer alongside a couple of killer hot sauces, curry pastes and other kitchen essentials. All products are made from homegrown and local produce, and Amanda's background in naturopathy inspires her soap-making practice. "We never intended it to be a real business, just a hobby, but we are so grateful for the way things have turned out," she says.

And on the interior? "It is just a collection of things that we have found over time," says Amanda. "Most of our furniture is from secondhand stores or Gumtree, we collect many cookbooks because we love food, and it turns out we really like the colour green."

Founder of Church Farm
General Store

•

Billinudgel,
NSW

"Most of our furniture is from secondhand stores or Gumtree, we collect many cookbooks because we love food, and it turns out we really like the colour green."

DANI DEAN

*From a mint-green kitchen
to bright and bold homewares,
this chic home pulls out all the stops.*

Just like the stunning spaces that stylist, florist, designer and business owner Dani Dean conceives for clients of her multidisciplinary creative studio, The Make Haus, she has created a gorgeous, colourful new home for herself and her young family on Sydney's Northern Beaches. In fact, Dani believes this project may be the highlight of a career that has included everything from creating beautiful weddings to reimagining retail spaces and homes.

The Dean house was previously owned by Dani's grandma, which meant she had already spent a great amount of time in it before its renovation. "I had pre-designed this space in my mind decades before it actually happened," she shares.

"When we first moved in we painted, opened the space, and updated the lighting. We were on a budget and the idea of renovating was daunting at that stage. Waiting five years before we embarked on the changes was the best move we made. Understanding how we used the house, the storage, the sunlight, and how we entertained and grew into the space were all key drivers in the updates," Dani says.

It has been enlivened with varying hues and is a lesson in using colour in the home in a refreshing and sophisticated way. "I really like to use colour in ways that don't feel overwhelming," she explains.

It's difficult to choose a favourite room as every space is chic and interesting. For Dani, the kitchen is the star of the show. "The kitchen anchors the home beautifully and really brings us joy." Here, mint-green joinery perfectly complements luxurious, oceanic-looking marble for an overall aesthetic that's modern and fresh.

"We are over the moon with the result and now have absolutely no regrets about going green."

Cool tones continue into the main bathroom with its deep-blue tiles and sage bath towels.

Moving to the welcoming living room you are greeted with a bevy of warm tones including turmeric and terracotta. A fluffy rug, timber furnishings and an upholstered sofa enhance the cosy vibe and make it an ideal spot to get comfortable on cooler days. The same toasty tones make their way to the primary bedroom, which features a wavy bouclé bedhead.

Stylist
+
Designer

•

Northern Beaches,
Sydney, NSW

221

"Creating furniture or wardrobe solutions that correctly store all your items improves the planning and enjoyment of our bedroom," Dani says. "Having bed linen that's easy to make and a killer throw and cushions also makes the bedroom feel more elevated."

And she offers an extra secret tip: "Generally, I love having baskets and secret storage so I can quickly convert the room if someone is coming over."

"Understanding how we used the house, the storage,
the sunlight, and how we entertained and grew
into the space were all key drivers in the updates."

RENOVATING ON A BUDGET

*We share some expert tips for how
you can make low-cost improvements
without breaking the bank.*

When it comes to renovating, most people aren't limited
by their imagination, but their budget. Whether you're
a first timer or a seasoned professional, the experience
can quickly become overwhelming without proper
planning and adequate resources to not only get the
job finished but also to a standard you'll be happy
to live with for years to come.

Here are a few cost-effective ways to approach your
next renovation project.

CONSULT YOUR IMAGE ARCHIVE.

Learning to save images you like before you've even picked up a power tool is crucial to the renovation process. This bank of images will be one you refer to, time and time again, not only to identify the common materials, colours, and tones that have stuck with you, but to keep your vision on track when you need to make decisions on the fly. The clearer your vision for your future home is, the more time- (and therefore cost-) efficient your build will be.

LOOK FOR COSMETIC FIXES FIRST.

Consider what can be done cosmetically before overhauling the layout of your home. Looking to let in more natural light? A lick of white paint and some strategically placed mirrors could do the trick. Is your kitchen a little tired but perfectly fine functionality-wise? Save money by replacing the cupboard doors and keeping the original carcass. If you can't achieve what you want through cosmetic updates alone, consider what changes you can make to your floor plan without relocating key plumbing or electrical outlets.

KNOW WHAT YOU CAN (REALISTICALLY) DO YOURSELF.

With a plethora of DIY tutorials available online, it's never been easier to teach yourself how to make improvements to your home. Painting, landscaping and decorating are all things you can confidently undertake yourself. But when it comes to waterproofing, electrical or plumbing, it's time to call in the experts. Any structural changes will also require a professional opinion, so be sure to build any of these services into your budget.

SOURCE SECONDHAND.

Not only are online marketplaces a great place to pick up well-priced furnishings and decor, they're a treasure trove of building materials and surplus goods. You'll often find excess tiles, reclaimed flooring, bathroom vanities – just about anything you might need to fit out your dream home. Make sure you can buy the quantity you need and always check measurements before purchasing.

CHOOSE TIMELESS FINISHES.

While you should absolutely put your own stamp on your space, think about the things that will be difficult to change if you ever tire of them. Tiles, for example, are expensive (and messy) to rip out and relay, while tapware can be changed relatively easily with the help of your plumber. Keeping surfaces timeless will ensure you get the most out of your investment with no regrets.

FAMILY HOMES

These beautiful abodes have been created and curated to meet the evolving needs of family life. From Courtney Adamo's renovated 120-year-old cottage in Bangalow to Tali Roth's metropolitan Melbournian masterpiece, these homes serve as the backdrop for life's most precious memories – all while proving that a space for nurturing a family can be as stylish as you'd like it to be.

JUSTINE CULLEN

*This light-filled house is home to a publishing
queen and her big, busy family.*

Justine Cullen is perhaps best known for launching *ELLE Australia* and spending five years there as the editor-in-chief, firmly establishing herself as a fashion tastemaker. Now, she's editor-in-chief of *InStyle* magazine, an ambassador for Cure Cancer, and published author.

Amid the pull of a demanding career and juggling four children, it's no wonder Justine's home is soothing and tranquil – a place of respite to retreat to at the end of a long day. The light-filled space in Sydney's beautiful Palm Beach echoes her effortlessly chic style, radiating the pared-back and refined aesthetic of her fashion choices.

Swathed in white on white, her waterside abode – which she shares with her husband and sons – is fresh and timeless. And while the interior colour palette may be led by neutrals, the home is filled with plenty of character with its stained-glass windows, exposed rafters, and coastal-style finishes.

There are plenty of special spaces in this home, but Justine's favourite is her bed nook. Drenched in sunlight, this charming alcove (and former sunroom) is accessed via a pair of ornate French doors. "The bed nook has a beautiful view over Pittwater in the day and a sky full of stars at night. It feels like you're sleeping in a treehouse," says Justine. The white-on-white aesthetic extends to the bedding, which Justine says is equally influenced by function and style. "The reason I love pure linen so much is because it looks good, even when the bed is unmade," she explains.

The house had been a holiday home for a long time and adjustments were needed to transform it into a permanent family home, such as improvements to heating and storage. However, from a style perspective, it was previously owned by a well-known interior designer, so there wasn't a lot to improve upon.

"We have four boys so I've just tried to keep it a pretty pared-back, calm, soothing space to counteract the crazy. And we've stuck with lots of white because it's the easiest to wash!" says Justine.

Editor

•

Palm Beach,
Sydney, NSW

231

"The bed nook has a beautiful view over
 Pittwater in the day and a sky full of stars at night.
 It feels like you're sleeping in a treehouse."

LIA TOWNSEND

A classic aesthetic and neutral palette allows
for changing accessories and stylised touches
in the home of this talented creative.

Grazing table stylist, cookbook author and Stories to Gather founder
Lia Townsend grew up in an Italian-Australian household, where long
lunches with family and friends regularly extended into the evening.
This love affair with food and its ability to bring people together inspired
her to create her own business, where she channels the same warmth
and energy into curating grazing tables and hampers. "Creating a sense
of occasion and bringing people together to share food is important
to me," she says.

There's an art to creating an impressive tablescape and Lia's
beautiful grazing spreads set the bar high. She uses seasonal produce
from epicurean artisans, beautiful floral arrangements, and chic table
decor to create whimsical and sophisticated settings that are tailored
to each occasion. "Each hamper and grazing table has a specific tone
and I really love bringing that to life for people to share," she says.

Her eye for detail extends to her home's chic interior, which
utilises a layered yet restrained neutral colour palette. "I keep the main
pieces in the home neutral so I can style them with different accessories
as my style shifts," she says. The current iteration is minimal and
deftly blends contemporary and classic decor. In the open-plan living
and dining room, upholstered seating in the form of a white linen
sofa and dining banquette keep things classic and comfortable, while
contemporary artworks, including a piece by Caroline Walls, add
a modern edge. Timber flooring carries throughout the apartment,
perfectly offsetting the white walls and bringing a sense of warmth
to the home.

There's a wonderful feeling of calm in the all-white primary
bedroom, which features classic wall panelling and pared-back decor.
Here, crisp white linen and a beautifully curved white bedhead make
for a dreamy spot to begin and end the day.

Lia and her husband have been renovating the house over
the years since moving in, and say the slower pace allows the spaces
to move and shift as they do. "During our time here I have learnt
the lesson of patience and to let the space evolve naturally rather
than doing everything when you first move in," says Lia. "The interior
has changed quite a lot. It is a reflection of my evolving style and the
dynamics of having a young child. It's very neutral now with easy-to-
clean surfaces (removable covers, wipeable bench seats etc.).
In general, I am drawn to a classic aesthetic."

Food stylist
+
Founder of Stories
to Gather

•

Rozelle,
Sydney, NSW

"I keep the main pieces in the home neutral so I can style them with different accessories as my style shifts."

LAUREN FREESTONE

Earthy tones, timbers and natural elements combine to create an elegant, simple and inspiring home for this Wiradjuri artist.

Warm and inviting, you simply want to spend hours lingering at the home of First Nations artist Lauren Freestone. Located in Newcastle on the New South Wales North Coast, the home backs onto bushland and is just like Lauren's paintings: earthy, elevated and understated.

When it comes to describing her interior style, Lauren says her aesthetic is "simple". She prefers to focus on earthy tones and natural elements to create a relaxed and warm atmosphere. You'll find plenty of woven rugs, cane armchairs and leather couches here, where the colour palette echoes the rust and terracotta linen on her bed. "Less is more for me," Lauren says.

In pride of place, though, are Lauren's artworks. The house is full of the artist's own work, as well as paintings by her father, also a celebrated Indigenous artist. The pair recently worked together on a mural, a meaningful and memorable experience for both. "My paintings definitely relate to who I am – they are about my family and our Wiradjuri history as well as our connection to Country, so they all tell a bit of my story."

Lauren has curated a family home that echoes her personal sense of style and identity, and says the act of making is who she is. "I have always been a creative person, I grew up watching my dad paint and exhibit his work. My grandfather made and sold Yidaki and boomerangs at the markets, so I guess it has always been a part of me."

Artist

•

Newcastle,
NSW

"My paintings definitely relate to who
I am – they are about my family and our
Wiradjuri history as well as our connection
to Country, so they all tell a bit of my story."

NATALIE FITCH

*The coastal home of a renowned jewellery
designer is an elegant and minimalist
oasis, with Scandi touches and brass finishes.*

Since launching Natalie Marie Jewellery in 2012, founder Natalie Fitch
has established herself as one of Australia's leading bespoke jewellery
designers. Synonymous with sentiment, sustainability, and authenticity,
Fitch crafts delicate, bespoke pieces that are at once striking and elegant.
And so it is when you step into her relaxed, yet refined home in Avalon
on Sydney's Northern Beaches.

A neutral colour palette of white and beige features throughout
her light-filled coastal home, with Scandinavian-inspired oak pieces
bringing a contemporary feel to the space. In the kitchen and bathroom,
brass finishings add an element of luxury to the crisp white subway
tiling, while in the living room a free-standing wood-burning fireplace
introduces a touch of rustic styling.

Soft white linen couches overflow with plush pillows, while potted
palms inject pops of green into the bedroom's lush colour scheme
of peaches and cream. Carefully curated and meticulously organised,
Natalie's home is a minimalist's dream.

"We live such busy lives. Home is most definitely a retreat for
us," says Natalie, who renovated the property inside and out to create
her and her husband's dream home. "We really wanted to create a home
that felt like a place of calm, somewhere that is light and fresh with
an open, airy feel. It's also a family home – we have two pets and
a toddler – so creating a space that feels comfortable and functional
was also really important."

Founder of Natalie
Marie Jewellery

•

Avalon,
Sydney, NSW

"We live such busy lives. Home
is most definitely a retreat for us."

SANTAL 26
MIES VAN DER ROHE
CHARLES & RAY EAMES
MARK ROTHKO
ABSTRACT EXPRESSIONISM
CASE STUDY HOUSES
TASCHEN

TALI ROTH

*Furniture, artwork and carefully chosen decor
pieces have transformed this generational home, bringing
Manhattan style to create a fresh family abode.*

In late 2020, interior designer Tali Roth and her husband and children moved into their new home – and they didn't change a thing. No renovations, no touch-ups, no little projects. Just straight into the space in Caulfield North, which used to belong to Tali's grandmother, who originally built it. After she sadly passed away, it was made available for Tali and her family, who had recently returned to Melbourne after living in New York for several years.

In just four months, Tali transformed the building into a family home, purely off the back of the furniture, artwork and decorating accents she already owned in New York. "I didn't know that we would be living here, so it's really all of my existing furniture from our life in New York simply rearranged," she explains. It's a testament to Tali's eye as a designer – in-demand with clients both in the US and at home – that she has been able to so seamlessly translate her Manhattan-cool interior style into a fresh and modern Melbourne home.

"I buy pieces I love rather than purchasing pieces just because they look good with something in my home or fit a particular space," Tali explains. It's the reason why, say, her glossy, vintage travertine coffee table looks as good in her new space as it did in the family's New York loft. The same goes for her collection of artwork, which includes a painting by Paul Davies. "Of course, you buy certain things that are specific over time, but the bulk should be 'love' pieces," she adds.

It's a good piece of advice, and one that she applies throughout her home, from the bedroom through to the airy living space with its portrait gallery hanging above the sofa – her favourite room in the house. Tali loves a "chic and serene" sleeping space, which she achieves by keeping the clutter away. Her top tips for styling a bedroom are to have sufficient storage to ensure there is no visual clutter, opt for neutral colours – "light or dark, depending on personal taste" (Tali prefers matching Bed Threads linen in white) – and symmetry. Oh, and the most important thing of all? "Make your bed every morning," she enthuses. "It's a must!"

Interior
designer

•

Caulfield North,
Melbourne, Victoria

"I buy pieces I love rather than
purchasing pieces just because
they look good with something in
my home or fit a particular space."

COURTNEY ADAMO

The dream home where this globetrotting family
settled, full of life, love and creativity.

If you followed lifestyle blogger Courtney Adamo on Instagram in 2015, you'll know that it was the year her life changed. It was the year that the Adamo family sold their London home and packed up their lives to travel the world for a year, homeschooling their five kids as they journeyed through the United States, Peru, Brazil, Chile, New Zealand, Australia, Japan, Sri Lanka and Italy.

It was on this trip that the Adamos first visited Byron Bay in northern New South Wales. They fell for the area's laidback lifestyle: surfing in the morning, hot coffee on the walk home, cooking family dinners in the evening under a syrupy Byron sunset. At the end of their sabbatical, the family of seven decided to leave London behind and put down permanent roots in Australia. They chose Bangalow, a town just outside of Byron, famous for its bustling farmer's market, and had been living there for some months before Courtney and her husband Michael spotted the house they now call home.

"I came to see it out of curiosity, with zero expectations," she recalls. "When I walked into the house, I felt immediately at home. Having lived in London for 12 years, always in old Victorian homes, I felt right at home in this old house with its creaky floors and old windows, tall ceilings, and rickety old doorknobs. I felt like I was being hugged."

Some pretty serious renovations were in order: the Adamos remodelled the house, moving the kitchen to the rear of the home so it would overlook the garden, and added a laundry room, second bathroom and one extra bedroom. In terms of decoration, Adamo went for simple, open and inviting, hanging the family's treasured pieces of art from their travels on every wall and letting in as much light as possible through big, open windows.

The result is an airy and relaxed family home, full of life and love. A place where kids can cook in the kitchen with their father, or grab a surfboard and head out to the beach. It's also where Courtney works, sitting at her little desk overlooking the garden and crafting e-courses on motherhood and pregnancy, or sharing snapshots of the family's life on Instagram.

"I wanted to create a home that felt unique to our family, with mementos from our travels, favourite art on the walls, favourite books on display, most-loved toys in baskets, plants in pots," she explains. "It gives me so much pleasure creating a place that feels like home to our family."

Lifestyle
blogger

•

Bangalow,
Northern NSW

255

"It gives me so much pleasure
creating a place that feels like
home to our family."

259

CREATING A SPACE THAT FEELS LIKE YOU

*How to design a home that exudes
your style and personality.*

Unravelling the secrets of what makes a space
somewhere you love to come home to is one
of the reasons why we first started *The Makers*.
With each home tour, we've witnessed first-hand
that a welcoming and well-styled interior is less
about collecting the latest designer pieces
or living in the fanciest home, and more about
a few thoughtful accents that inject personality
into a space.

Here's how you too can bring your own
personal style into your home.

DON'T RUSH IT.

While it can be tempting to quickly fill an empty space so your home feels finished, you're guaranteed to give your home more character with objects and furnishings collected over time. The layered, cosy look found in so many of the homes featured on *The Makers* is a culmination of pieces amassed at different times and places. Some new, some upcycled or antique, all assembled to create an overall composition that's deeply personal.

DESIGN FOR THE WAY YOU WISH TO LIVE.

How you set up your home will ultimately set the tone for how you spend your day to day. Spend some time thinking about what you want from your home and how it can best serve you. Love reading? Create an inviting reading nook or equip your bedside table with proper lighting and a fresh stack of books. Is conversing over family meals your favourite part of the day? Invest in an accommodating dining table and position it away from the television or other distractions. Maybe you want to challenge yourself to cook different cuisines? Keep a few new cookbooks in your kitchen as a reminder. You'll be surprised how much a few small changes will make your home feel like a true reflection of you.

DISPLAY YOUR FAVOURITE OBJECTS.

Open up those cupboards and dust off any objects you might've picked up over the years – either on travels, passed down from family, or purchased just because. Now consider where they could live in view every day, either perched on a shelf, coffee table or (in the case of decorative plates or utensils) mounted on a wall. The idea is not to clutter or crowd your space, but selectively decorate your home with a few things you absolutely love that tell a little of your own personal story.

INVEST IN QUALITY PIECES TO KEEP.

A few familiar pieces go a long way to creating a homely vibe. While it's not always possible to have all your furniture follow your every move, taking some treasured items from one place to the next will instantly make you feel settled. Quality bed linens are one such thing – they'll not only ensure you stay comfortable and well-rested for years to come, but make anywhere you take them feel like home.

COUNTRY ESCAPES

Set away from the clamour of city life, these
country retreats, and the designers, artists
and renovators who envisioned them, work
with nature to create serene spaces that settle
harmoniously into their surroundings. Each
a uniquely idyllic paradise, these peaceful places
provide fertile ground to nurture the creativity
of the inhabitants within.

EMMA LANE

*A love affair with Spain is the
story behind this sprawling
country homestead.*

As far as dream homes go, entrepreneur Emma Lane's is top of the list. Her sprawling property dubbed The Range, in the Byron Bay Hinterland in far-northern New South Wales, is set on 120 acres of land and boasts idyllic views of rolling hills and gorgeous coastline. The property encompasses Emma's own family home (the homestead), as well as two spaces for holiday accommodation (the barn and the cabin), for those looking to immerse themselves in a rich architectural space and stunning natural surrounds.

Emma's career began in advertising and has seen her go on to help many brands with name generation, logo creation and marketing strategy. Now, Emma creates destination lifestyle brands with her husband Tom through The Lane Estates. The pair are the brains behind the much-loved The Farm Byron Bay and The Beach House East Coast in Ballina, where sustainability and design are equally important driving forces. "All our projects tend to have an element of sustainability and a giving back aspect somehow to environment or community," Emma shares.

The Range home was created by a team of dedicated creatives including architect friend Dominic Finlay Jones of DFJ Architecture. "We pretty much kept a slab and a few walls and re-built from there," recalls Emma. Dominic travelled with Emma and her family to Spain to get design inspiration from the local architecture. "We had spent some time living in Spain and loved the Spanish architecture, so we used this inspiration to merge with our Australian lifestyle and I think what we ended up with was a perfect blend of both," says Emma.

Stucco walls, arches, natural materials, and a warm, neutral colour palette prevail in the homestead and play into the Spanish aesthetic. The home embraces rich decorative details albeit in a pared-back way as Emma likes to "keep it elegant and simple".

Every space in this home has been thoughtfully created, but the living room (Emma's favourite) is the showstopper. In this inviting open-plan space, a large stone fireplace sits at the helm of a textured sunken living room, which is positioned to take advantage of the sweeping hinterland views. It's nothing short of spectacular.

Creative
+
Founder of
The Lane Estates

•

Byron Bay Hinterland,
NSW

265

"We had spent some time living in Spain
and loved the Spanish architecture,
so we used this inspiration to merge
with our Australian lifestyle."

The 20TH CENTURY ART BOOK

The WEST

Encyclopedia of Art

AMERICAN INDIAN ART

KELSEY COPPETTI

Check in to this unique rental property,
decorated with calming neutrals and organic
textures inspired by the surrounding desert.

Celebrated for its distinct trees and mesmerising sunrises and sunsets, Joshua Tree has become an increasingly popular holiday destination over the past few decades. There is no shortage of Airbnbs in the national park, so for interior designer Kelsey Coppetti, creating a unique property was of the utmost importance.

Alongside partner Dustyn, who is the other half of their company Studio Marrant, she sensitively restored a once-abandoned desert home into an ultra-chic Airbnb. "We were looking for a home in Joshua Tree that felt very immersed in the surrounding desert – something that truly felt unique in a sea of ever-growing cookie-cutter type Airbnbs and short-term rentals," she says.

The property was the catalyst for starting their company. "When we purchased the property that is now Arro Dunes, it was with the intention we'd use it as a jumping-off point for an interior design and creative studio and pour our creative hearts into the space." Kelsey had previously worked in digital agencies and marketing but had always invested in good design on the side. She decided to take the plunge and create a hospitality space that could be shared with others.

The pair completely gutted the house that sits on 10 unfenced acres, overlaying it with a desert-meets-wabi-sabi design that's also refreshingly modern. A neutral palette and smart use of organic textures can be seen inside, with stucco walls, woven rugs, timber furniture and wooden ceiling beams. "We wanted to honour the desert elements surrounding the house with palette-similar organic and natural objects inside," she says.

"We're very hands-on with the entire process, so if we can't find the right furniture piece, we'll make it ourselves or we'll build our own custom millwork pieces, entirely landscape a yard, weld our own planter beds and fence, or refurbish old windows."

Interior
designer

•

Joshua Tree,
California, United States

271

Kelsey has a decade of experience with ceramics and has peppered the home with her own sculpture and lamp designs. The abode has also been decorated with antiques, which bring added character to the space, with a mix of old and new.

"We ride a fine line of old things we probably shouldn't put in a high-traffic Airbnb but so far we've only had appreciation from guests who have respect for the space. Antiques bring so much warmth, depth and a room full of stories, that they're almost a non-negotiable for me when designing," she says.

White linen introduces a fresh and clean look to the primary bedroom, while French doors provide a connection to the outdoors where guests can unwind on the timber deck under the pristine Joshua Tree sky.

"We wanted to honour the desert
elements surrounding the house
with palette-similar organic
and natural objects inside."

SARA COMBS

*Design and nature come together in this
renovated hacienda home, a desert oasis
for relaxing and recharging.*

Sara Combs is the one of the brains behind The Joshua Tree House,
a collection of luxurious yet relaxed homes for people to reflect, reset
and create in. The idea was born out of Sara and her husband's desire
to have a creative space to recharge in nature. The property that
kickstarted the business is aptly located in Joshua Tree and serves
as an oasis in the desert.

    "I love to start [renovating] by getting to know the existing
structure and surrounding landscape," she says. "Then I apply that
mood to basic functionalities of a home. I start with the most ordinary
experiences – sleeping, eating, bathing – and begin to design around
those moments. These everyday things make up the majority of our
lives, so I love to design for them in the hope of transforming the
ordinary into something special. Incorporating natural materials into
each space is an important element as well. I want to design spaces
that are not afraid to be lived in, so I look for natural materials to wear
in beautifully and get better with age."

    The renovated 1949 hacienda home embraces a Spanish-meets-
Moroccan aesthetic, celebrating design and nature. Warm hues that
mimic the surrounding landscape dominate the interior colour palette,
from the rust-toned sofa in the open-plan living area to the turmeric
linen in the main bedroom. Potted cacti have been dotted throughout
the house to blur the line between home and nature.

    "Part of what we loved so much about this house were the
many windows looking out to hundreds of acres of untouched desert
landscape," Sara says. "We really wanted to blend the interior design
with the landscape as much as possible by bringing natural elements
and colours inside, and by creating outdoor living spaces."

    Timber brings an abundance of warmth, from the rattan chairs,
bed frame, exposed ceiling beams and kitchen island to the rustic
dining table, which was made with repurposed wood pulled from the
walls during the renovation. Patterned rugs and upholstery play into
the Moroccan style and inject the home with personality and interest.
Outside, a hot tub surrounded by more than 100 Joshua trees is the
perfect spot to unwind, taking in the natural surrounding and
exquisite sunsets.

Designer

•

Joshua Tree,
California, United States

Sara shares her top tip for a well-styled home: "It's all about creating spaces that are connected to their environment, designing for comfort and everyday life and incorporating nature both through plants and natural materials.

"When it comes to designing a bedroom, a comfortable bed is my number-one priority. It's all about a good mattress and pillows, cosy sheets and blankets. A good night of sleep is such a simple concept but is a true game changer."

HANNAH SINDORF

*This home in an artist colony is a creative sanctuary
that reflects the Hispanic craftsmanship of the area.*

Hannah Sindorf believes that finding her home in Taos, New Mexico
was nothing short of fate. "It was the space I had been dreaming of –
I gasped when I saw the photos online," says the jeweller and founder
of Halcyon. "Even though it was more than I could afford at the time,
something in me intuitively knew that this was the right place and time."

With that, the creative packed up her life on the East Coast and
moved to the historic artist colony in northern New Mexico. "Taos had
been on my mind for a long time," she adds. "The house I envisioned
living in was the house that popped up on Craigslist when I was in dire
need of a sanctuary."

Thanks to her built-in jewellery studio, warm terracotta linen,
and a treasure trove of family heirlooms, the rental quickly felt like
home to Hannah. It currently houses countless sculptures fashioned
by her late father, precious photos of family members, and vintage
furniture originally purchased by her grandparents in the 1950s.
"I'd like to think my style travels with me," she shares. "I have
so many pieces that I will keep forever because they're timeless
and have great sentimental value."

"I've been creating since I was very young. I was lucky to grow
up with creative parents who always encouraged me to pursue
whatever I was interested in making, whether it was drawing,
painting or woodwork. It's been a part of me for a long time. I find
when I'm not working on my jewellery, I feel like I'm missing part
of my happiness. I don't think I've gone more than a week without
sitting at my bench since I started seven years ago. Producing
something beautiful brings me joy, so I try to do it as often as possible."

She hopes that her handcrafted bracelets, rings, necklaces and
earrings bring similar joy and sentimental value to her cherished
customers. "My website says 'handmade with love and intention',
because that's really what I try to do," she adds. "I think my customers
can feel it when they receive their jewellery."

Jeweller

•

Taos, New Mexico,
United States

Her favourite room in the house is her bedroom. "Having a kiva fireplace in the bedroom is so luxurious and cosy in the winter. I also just love being in bed and relaxing at the end of the day – having a simple, clean, comfortable bedroom is really important to me.

"Having a space that's a reflection of you and what you love is my best advice. It's not about what's trendy, it's about having a collection of objects that pull you in and bring you joy. That's what will ultimately make a space feel like home."

"I'd like to think my style
 travels with me."

ANTHONY D'ARGENZIO

Inside a century-old home turned luxury retreat
and destination rental by a clever creative.

For real estate and design aficionado Anthony D'Argenzio, transforming properties into destination rentals is one part of his enviable day-to-day job. One of his most notable projects is the exquisite This Old Hudson Maison, located almost two hours outside Manhattan in the Hudson Valley, New York.

"For creating interiors, I like to start by outlining my goals," he says. "Once I have my outline, I will have a creative brainstorm and make a moodboard before I execute. What drew me to the house was the old-world charm. I wanted people to find their own version of that experience when they visited This Old Hudson, the kind of place where creativity blooms and art happens on the spot."

Anthony is the founder of Zio and Sons, a bespoke design, creative services and photography studio in New York City and the Hudson Valley. He began his career as a set and prop stylist before transitioning into interiors and lifestyle design, and eventually into the real estate world where he now transforms properties into luxurious destination rentals.

This Old Hudson Maison has a distinct old-world European feel to it. Step inside and you're immediately transported to the French countryside, with each room dotted with carefully curated vintage and antique pieces. "I wanted the space to feel luxurious but also comfortable and lived-in," Anthony says. The original wallpaper, which features a beautifully ornate design, was the starting point for the home's overall interior scheme.

The rustic-meets-upstate kitchen boasts charm in spades with its farmhouse-style sink, gold tapware, antique cupboard, and decorative terracotta-hued wall tiles. The tiles carry through to the bathroom which has a similar chic farmhouse aesthetic, while the living areas exude a romantic feel with upholstered seating and patina finishes.

His top tips for a well-styled bedroom? "Less is more in a bedroom. Always start with good bedding – a very important element for any sleeping space – and build a space that is just as comfortable. I like to think about how I am going to use the room. What are the design features or objects that will continue to inspire me every day?"

Interior designer
+
Real estate

•

Hudson Valley,
New York, United States

"I wanted the space to feel
luxurious but also comfortable
and lived-in."

LYNDA GARDENER

*An old driveway was transformed
into dreamy boutique accommodation
by a visionary interior designer.*

In 2021, Lynda Gardener snapped up a slice of land, a driveway in fact, located next door to The White House, her boutique accommodation in Daylesford, Victoria. "Very spontaneous, to be honest," she recalls. "Quite mad!" But she had the spark of an idea to create something from the ground up, her first ever new build, working with limited land size and space.

The result is Room + Board, holiday accommodation for a couple or a single person looking to lounge around and generally just relax. With no doors – except for those leading to the pod bathroom – the space is designed to be open and inviting, with plenty of light and airflow to promote relaxation. "Light, bright and calm to the eyes," Lynda explains of her thought process when designing the interior. Big windows look out over plentiful space, and barn-style doors open into the garden at the front and the rear of the building. All the furniture, from the cosy, linen-upholstered bed to the low couches in the living area, were chosen to be close to the ground.

"I specifically wanted [that]," Lynda explains. "It's a lounge-y space to just relax, read, talk, laze about or just be." This same feeling carries through from the open-plan living area – which backs onto a well-appointed kitchen – right into the bedroom. "I want all my homes to feel as though you can literally run and jump in and curl up on anything you choose," she adds.

Lynda says she loves designing boutique accommodation properties because it gives her the freedom to create whatever she is in the mood for. "Each property gives me the opportunity to realise something individual all over again. I enjoy making my spaces warm, welcoming and cosy for people to escape to."

Interior designer

•

Daylesford, Victoria

301

"It really makes me so happy to know there are so many guests who enjoy all the elements I bring to a space and what I have created. I always add many personal items, from my collections and art, so all of the homes are very personal to me and I feel that my guests love that too. It's an environment that instantly feels cosy and you just don't want to leave."

She credits staying focused, having fun and learning from her mistakes as a recipe for success. And her top tips for a well-styled bedroom and home? "Lots of layers and textures, and keeping to a colour palette that suits not just the room but the entire home. The beds are so important to me: colour, texture, layers. Pure linen always. A throw or two and roughly styled scatter cushions, quite relaxed and loose."

"Each property gives me the opportunity
to create something individual all over again.
I enjoy making my spaces warm, welcoming
and cosy for people to escape to."

SIMONE HAAG

*This relaxed beachfront weekender is a family heirloom
that has been transformed through the generations.*

When Melbourne-based interior designer Simone Haag first visited
Phillip Island almost a decade ago with her now-husband Rhys,
she didn't expect she would ever own property there.

However, over the years, Simone and Rhys made frequent trips
back to the island – always staying at Rhys' parents' property, dubbed
Angler's Shack – and they soon fell in love with the area. After their
wedding, the couple often scouted the locale for their own beach house,
but could never find anything quite like Rhys' family cottage. So, when
Simone's in-laws decided to move to a more retirement-worthy place,
Simone and Rhys jumped at the opportunity to make Angler's Shack
their own and keep the home in the family – as well as all the memories
they had made there.

"The property holds a lot of sentimental value and we were
so grateful to be able to keep the shack in the family. Also, the location
is perfect. Over the years as we made regular trips to the shack and our
relationship turned into something more serious, it just became a place
very close to our hearts," she says.

Simone took advantage of the simple layout of the home, making
small updates to the space as opposed to major renovations. Cabinets
were repositioned, the kitchen bench was retiled, and the floors were
given a fresh lick of paint. Aside from that, Simone did what she does
best – used decor pieces such as furniture, art, ceramics and lighting,
to give the home a fresh personality. Remaining committed to an
olive, charcoal and tangerine colour palette throughout, there are
many vintage and globally sourced finds that have been thoughtfully
positioned around the home. The result? A Californian bungalow vibe
that exudes warmth and comfort.

"I always start my creative process with things I actually love,"
Simone says, "so I don't design the space and then fill it; instead, I find
the things I want and then design the space around them. For Angler's
Shack, I was certain I wanted to create a California-Arizona vibe and
approached the design process with this in mind.

"I had already collected a few pieces before we even purchased
the shack, including the most amazing Bumling pendant from Sweden,
which now hangs over the dining table, as well as beautiful tangerine
Carl Hansen dining chairs."

Interior designer

•

Phillip Island,
Victoria

307

Located only an hour-and-a-half drive away from the couple's Ringwood residence in Melbourne and a stone's throw from the beach, Simone has created a breathtaking weekender. It's a sanctuary reminiscent of the perfect Australian holiday retreat – one she knows will continue to remain a family heirloom where memories are made and laughter is shared.

"For me, updating the space is something I'm never going to set and forget. It's a constant process of layering items, adding pieces, changing things in the rooms – it's never complete for me so I'm always looking to add more."

309

"I always start my creative process
with things I actually love."

ALLIE CAMERON

*A mid-century modern den
straight out of the 1960s.*

During her high-school years, creative Allie Cameron started her own small business where she would find and sell vintage and secondhand fashion pieces online. It was during this time and after her travels to India that she became acutely aware of the environmental impacts the fashion industry has on the planet, and she decided she wanted to be part of the change. Enter HARA The Label, the sustainable Melbourne-based clothing label Allie founded at just 23 years of age.

HARA The Label uses natural dyes and bamboo fabric to create a soft range of underwear, loungewear and sportswear. Every step of the process from cut to dispatch is conducted from their Melbourne factory and the brand has teamed up with the Environmental Justice Foundation to support their environmental projects. They are working on new products for men and non-binary people as well as a maternity range. Allie has also launched a beauty brand, Hinu, which focuses on using natural ingredients for hair care.

As far as her home base goes, Allie was introduced to her 1960s Torquay home by a friend. "I would stay occasionally, house sitting and visiting over the course of a few years until eventually a spot became open and I took it straight away," she says. Surrounded by lush greenery and situated by a creek, this home feels warm and welcoming thanks to timber cladding and a wood-burning fireplace in the living area. "I really wanted to embrace the timber features and all the small original details that this little '60s gem already had, so I slowly collected vintage pieces from stores, Facebook Marketplace and op shops," says Allie.

In the best way possible, this home almost looks as though it hasn't been touched since the 1960s. Adding to the delightfully nostalgic vibe are decorative yellow and green patterned kitchen tiles, which inject the space with colour and retro charm. These hues can be seen throughout the interior styling palette, from the Marianne Roussety artwork in the dining area to the olive-green linen in the bedroom. Vintage furniture and decor are peppered throughout, including bentwood dining chairs and a tan Togo occasional chair. It's a space that is at once thoughtfully curated and entirely lived-in. "I always want guests to feel cosy and welcomed instead of being worried they'll dirty, break or misplace something," she says.

Sustainable
fashion designer
+
Founder of
HARA The Label

•

Torquay,
Victoria

"I always want guests to feel cosy and welcomed instead of being worried they'll dirty, break or misplace something."

JAI VASICEK

*A love for all things theatrical
was the guiding inspiration behind this
maximalist dream home.*

When artist Jai Vasicek met his partner Matt, a filmmaker, the couple
bonded over their shared love of film, art, fashion and culture. This
love for all things theatrical would go on to inform their life together.
It's the guiding inspiration, too, behind their maximalist dream home
in Brunswick Heads in northern New South Wales, and the reason
for several of their decorating choices.

   "This space takes me back to the spaces of Europe," Jai explains.
Those scenes that remind him of cinematic, Luhrmann-esque settings:
wide, tiled terraces overlooking greenery; an antique-filled kitchen
with a cherry-red tiled splashback; a ceiling plastered with a decorative
motif. "When you enter our place you feel a presence that is very global,"
the artist says. "Every door and window is from somewhere other than
Australia. It feels amazing to live in Australia and feel like I'm in Europe."

   The whole house has been decorated with this unique sensibility
in mind. "It is our belief that every piece of furniture should activate
you with a memory or a good feeling. Not just a trend." Take, for
instance, the artwork by Stan Piechaczek, a piece called 'I've Got Your
Back' – "it represents our relationship," says Jai. "So every day I see it,
it just puts a smile on my face."

   Jai's artistic practice, which began with paintings, now sees him
dabble in ceramics and fashion.

   "Everything I make is really some facet of me – the personality
that I am. The act of making by going for it inspires other people.
I'm super 'loud' with my work but very 'shy' with the procedure and
the creative process. From making to exhibiting is a way that I express
myself. Making really is who I am and what I make reflects where
I have been and travelled to and also how I'm feeling," he says.

   "I am still learning every day. I love navigating, even through
problem solving, because it brings you closer to yourself. I'm starting
to be around some incredible people who are wanting to collaborate
and this extends into other things I'm interested in exploring, such
as film and fashion."

Creative
+
Artist

•

Brunswick Heads,
NSW

When Jai comes home he likes to feel renewed for the next day's creative work. This is why the styling of the bedroom is so important in creating the right mood. "I find patterns and prints hectic when it comes to my bed," he explains. "I sometimes think simple is the best – it keeps your mind quiet... I think your bed needs to always feel like a new canvas every day."

323

"When you enter our place you feel
a presence that is very global.
It feels amazing to live in Australia
and feel like I'm in Europe."

SYLVIE KETTLE

*This artist has transformed an old garlic
drying shed on her family farm into a charming
cottage where inspiration abounds.*

Sylvie Kettle's dreamy abstract paintings are imbued with feminine
energy and the serene calm of natural landscapes. The young artist has
been painting since she was eight years old – she grew up on coastal
farmland and says painting is the overflow of who she is. "Being
a creative, there really is no separation between your personality
and the urge to create worlds. Painting isn't just what I do for work,
it's a symptom of my whole being," she says.

With art so central to all she does, the first thing Sylvie did
after moving into her home was to renovate her studio. "It actually
used to be an old garlic drying shed here at Farm & Co, so I had
it renovated into a sweet cottage vibe with vintage French windows
and doors. It was beautiful watching the space come to life with a bit
of love and intention."

When it comes to styling, the artist likes anything that has character.
"Sometimes, I invent full personalities around things in the house,"
she laughs. "My favourite pieces are my green velvet, mid-century
couch and a 100-year-old African milking stool that was carved from
one piece of wood. It's so beautiful."

Whether she is curating art, design pieces or furniture for her
home, Sylvie says she is guided by authenticity. "Everything carries its
own vibration, so I guess it's about featuring pieces that truly resonate
with you rather than buying generic and mass-produced things," says
Sylvie. "This is why art is so unique. It honestly blows my mind to think
of the purity of artistic creation; it can't be manufactured. Anything
created with artistic intention will bring its own essence to your space."

And when it comes to a favourite space or part of the house,
Sylvie says the front porch and grassy lawn is where she can
immerse herself in the landscape. "I have a special Saturday ritual
when I come back from the beach to laze around on blankets
on the lawn and watch the clouds go by. I also often stargaze with
my beautiful neighbours."

Artist

•

Cudgen,
NSW

"Anything created with artistic intention will bring its own essence to your space."

ZOE YOUNG

*This rustic cottage is a light-filled artist's
paradise and cherished family home.*

Nestled in the Southern Highlands of New South Wales is the airy,
light-filled cottage that artist Zoe Young calls home. It's ideally situated:
isolated enough that the painter has both the physical and mental space
to create her incredible, emotive artworks, but close enough to the
nearby woods that she can duck out on a sunny day to pick fresh apples
before returning to her studio – where she's often been since dawn –
to continue her work.

It's idyllic here, in this magical place where Zoe and her family
have lived for more than five years. When they first moved in, they
painted everything white – inspired by Wendy Whiteley's stark, blank-
canvas house – and did quite a bit of renovation work. They opened up
the kitchen so the space flowed and removed "a lot of faux finishes and
bad lino".

The end result is a lived-in and organic space, perfect for an artist,
a horticulturist (Zoe's husband Reg) and their two children, who love
to skateboard through the house or indulge in a game of handball.
"With young children and animals in tow, we've never wanted anything
precious," Zoe explains. "The garden is cascading and rambling so the
house is just simple and bright, to honour the things we've collected
over the years."

Among Zoe's prized possessions are the heirloom drinks trolley
inherited from her grandmother and her collection of exquisite coffee
cups by ceramicist Kate McKay. "To me, that's luxury," she enthuses.
"To have handmade everyday objects." There are even specialty hooks
by architect Willea Ferris on the walls, and artworks by Zoe's grandfather
and, of course, herself, dotted around the space.

Everything in the cottage is curated according to Zoe's interior
design creed of simplicity, efficiency and light. This is especially evident
in her bedroom, where the high ceilings, huge windows and white-
panelled walls are given the chance to shine with minimal styling.
It's a tranquil space where the artist comes to rest after long days
in the studio. "Keep it simple," she advises, when decorating a space.
"Have everyday rituals to keep it bright and clean, and only have what
you love around you."

Artist

•

Bowral,
NSW

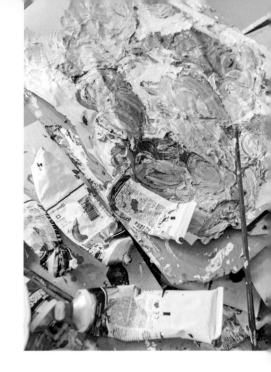

334

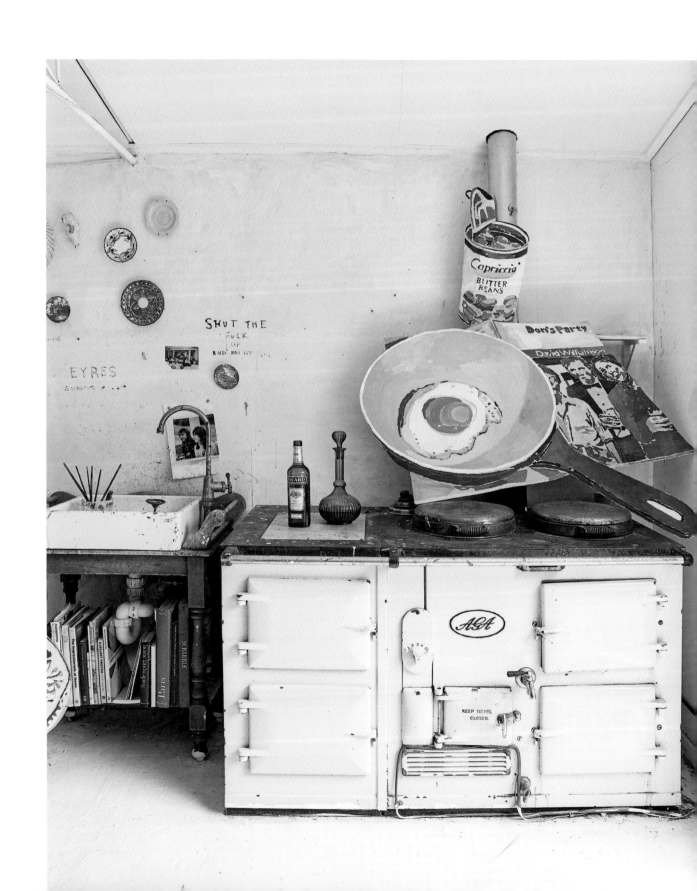

"To me, that's luxury, to have handmade everyday objects."

THANK YOU

TO OUR TALENTED CONTRIBUTORS

To every Maker who features in this book, you graciously welcomed us into your homes and inspired us with your creativity, ideas and style. Thank you for having us, for sharing the spaces you have so cleverly and lovingly designed, and trusting us with the special places you call your own.

TO OUR SHOOT TEAMS

We count ourselves incredibly lucky to work with talented photographers and stylists across the globe, from Sydney to London to New York and beyond. Thank you to our photographers Victoria Adamson, Hannah Blackmore, Alaina Bradshaw, Becca Crawford, Alisha Gore, Victoria Jane, Alana Landsberry, Meghan Marin, Benito Martin, Bethany Nauert, Jenna Peffley, Jessie Prince and Amelia Stanwix for capturing the homes so skillfully, and to our stylists Beck Simon, Laura Woolf, Audrey Won, Sami Simper, Hannah Simmons, Melete Finch, Paige Anderson, Sarah Ellison, Brady Tolbert, Paige Wassel, Danielle Armstrong, Corina Koch, Anna Delprat, Rory Carter and Jackie Brown, for your exceptional taste and talent.

TO OUR WRITERS

Melissa King, Hannah-Rose Yee, Rachael Thompson, Alexandra English and Juna Xu: we are so grateful for your thoughtful words and features. Thank you.

TO OUR PUBLISHING TEAM

To Evi O., Susan Le, Pamela Sarly, Pru Engel, Lucy Heaver, Rachel Carter and the whole team at Evi-O.Studio – this would not have been possible without your energy for our vision. Thank you for helping us bring our Makers series to life. To our in-house team – Stephanie Squadrito (who has been the driving force behind our Makers series since the beginning, pressing publish on our very first home tour and iterating the series time and time again), Melissa King (who works tirelessly to not only ensure we have an ultra-inspiring tour to publish each Sunday, but that each home and feature is presented perfectly), Rachael Thompson (who has interviewed countless Makers for the Bed Threads Journal and puts words to the beautiful spaces each and every Maker creates), Bella Westaway (for doing read-through after read-through in your first month on the job at Bed Threads) and Karina Camenzind (who has gone above and beyond to make sure every single image, feature and home tour sings in this book – without you, we'd still be without a first draft).

AND MOST OF ALL... TO THE BED THREADS COMMUNITY

To our loyal customers, readers and followers, this is for you. You inspire us more than you'll ever know. Everything we do, we do for you. Thank you for welcoming us into your homes with open arms, believing in us and supporting Bed Threads. It means everything to us.

THIS EDITION PUBLISHED IN 2024 BY HARDIE GRANT BOOKS, AN IMPRINT OF HARDIE GRANT PUBLISHING
FIRST PUBLISHED IN 2023 BY BED THREADS

Hardie Grant Books (Melbourne)
Wurundjeri Country
Building 1, 658 Church Street
Richmond, Victoria 3121

Hardie Grant North America
2912 Telegraph Ave
Berkeley, California 94705

hardiegrant.com/books

Hardie Grant acknowledges the Traditional Owners of the Country on which we work, the
Wurundjeri People of the Kulin Nation and the Gadigal People of the Eora Nation, and recognises
their continuing connection to the land, waters and culture. We pay our respects to their Elders past
and present.

PHOTOGRAPHY ©
Victoria Adamson: pp. 174–179
Hannah Blackmore: pp. 33–35, 118–121
Alaina Bradshaw: pp. 102–105
Becca Crawford: pp. 180–187, 314–319
Alisha Gore: pp. 136–141, 220–225, 230–237, 238–241
Victoria Jane: pp. 100–101
Alana Landsberry: pp. 12–17, 18–21, 22–27, 242–245, 332–337
Meghan Marin: pp. 76–81, 86–93, 94–101, 106–109, 294–299
Benito Martin: pp. 132–135, 154–159, 160–165, 246–249, 264–269, 326–331
Bethany Nauert: pp. 114–117, 270–277, 278–285
Jenna Peffley: pp. 50–57, 58–65, 66–71, 72–75, 286–293
Jessie Prince: pp. 212–219, 254–259, 320–325
Amelia Stanwix: pp. 28–31, 36–39, 40–43, 44–49, 110–113, 122–127, 142–147, 148–153

The Makers.
ISBN 9781761450846

10 9 8 7 6 5 4 3 2

ART DIRECTION & DESIGN — Evi-O.Studio | Susan Le
ILLUSTRATION & TYPESETTING — Evi-O.Studio | Katherine Zhang
PHOTOGRAPHY — Victoria Adamson, Hannah Blackmore,
Alaina Bradshaw, Becca Crawford, Alisha Gore, Victoria Jane,
Alana Landsberry, Meghan Marin, Benito Martin, Bethany Nauert,
Jenna Peffley, Jessie Prince and Amelia Stanwix
COPY EDITORS — Pru Engel, Shannon Harley
PROOFREADERS — Rachel Carter, Lucy Heaver

PRE-PRODUCTION — Colour reproduction by Splitting Image Colour Studio.
PRINTING — Printed in China through Asia Pacific Offset.

Bed
Threads.